THE LOVE OF CHRIST
IN THE LOCAL CONGREGATION:

Sharing Together

In The

Life And Labor

Of Jesus

Larry Deason

Life Communications™
Lady Lake, FL

Unless otherwise noted, all Scripture
quotations are from the
New International Version.

Previously published as *The Love of Christ in the
Local Congregation* (©1987), *The Life of Christ We
Share: Members One of Another* (©1988), and *The
Labor of Christ Through Us: Every Member a Min-
ister* (©1988), all by Life Communications.™

First Printing 1987
Revised Printing 1993
Second Printing 1998
Third Printing 2007

THE LOVE OF CHRIST IN THE LOCAL CONGREGATION

OTHER BOOKS

by

Larry Deason:

The Eternal Purpose and Plan of God:
The Meaning and Purpose of Life

That You May Have Life:
Gospel of John

The Righteousness of God:
Romans

One Step Closer to Jesus:
Losing Life, Finding Life

Broken Off Flowers & Blown Out Candles:
Finding Wholeness Through Brokenness

Set Free? Stay Free!
(The Fallacy and Failure of Legalism)

CONTENTS (CONTINUED)

Part Three

The Labor of Christ Through Us: Every Member a Minister

CONTENTS

CONTENTS (CONTINUED)

Part Two

The Life of Christ We Share: Members One of Another

Acknowledgements

I owe a great debt of gratitude to many people for the encouragement and support that has been given me in my attempt to write.

I am especially grateful to those who have been a "hands on" part of this writing and the other books. Without these friends in Christ this work of faith could not have been accomplished:

To the late Norma West, my secretary, who typed all the transcripts and manuscripts. To Bill Bean and Susan Ziomek, who took the rough drafts and, by hours of editing, put it all together in a readable style. And to Steve Singleton, Keith Luker, and Dick Girard, who did the final word processing and computer lay-out work before sending it to the printer.

With these fellow-workers who have shared, from their hearts, this "labor of love" with me, I from the depths of my being thank our Lord Jesus Christ that we all are "members one of another."

PREFACE

In offering this revised edition of my trilogy of biblical studies concerning relationships among the people of God, I am reminded of the question posed to the prophet Ezekiel: "Can these bones live?"

The first division in this series may be likened to the skeletal structure of the whole body of teaching;[1] the second, to the "meat on the bones";[2] and the final piece, to the breath of life that (I trust) will make the biblical teaching "come alive" in the midst of the Christian community.[3] Or, to trade a biological analogy for an architectural one, we can view love as the foundation of the structure, the sharing of life as its framework, and mutual ministry as its completing superstructure.

For those familiar with this series, an inevitable amount of overlapping will be noted in the concepts presented. I have tried to maintain clarity and continuity of content from part to part without being unnecessarily redundant. Each of the three major divisions contributes to a complete course of study that logically builds from the foundation of God's love to the goal of God's people serving one another; yet, each stands complete in itself.

---

[1]Larry Deason, *The Love of Christ in the Local Congregation* (Clifton Park, NY: Life Communications, 1987).

[2]Larry Deason, *The Life of Christ We Share: Members One of Another* (Clifton Park, NY: Life Communications, 1988).

[3]Larry Deason, *The Labor of Christ Through Us: Every Member a Minister* (Clifton Park, NY: Life Communications, 1988).

ix

Introductory Reflections:
Part One

It's been over twenty-five years since I seriously began to study and teach God's Word. In those early years, I would come home from school to my local congregation and would be asked to preach. When I would ask my parents, "What would you like for me to speak about next Sunday?", my mother would say, "Why don't you talk about love?" At the time, I wasn't impressed with her suggestion. I thought there were more important things in God's revealed Word to preach than that thing called love.

Now I know better. Nothing is more important than love... God's love. He has called us all to know and learn this love. As members of the Body of Christ, we are called to know, learn, become, and express this love in all of our relationships.

Loving as God does is what this book is all about. I have attempted to point out the most important need as well as the greatest challenge to us who claim to follow Christ and to be members of His Body, the Church: to love as Christ, our Lord and Savior, loves.

Larry Deason

2

Part One

The Love Of Christ

In The

Local Congregation

*"The priority of any local church
must be love,
because love is the basic
identifying characteristic
of the New Testament church."*

1

THE DISTINCTIVENESS AND IMPORTANCE OF THE LOCAL CHURCH

"Ecclesiology" is the proper name for that field of biblical study which deals with doctrine pertaining to the church. This book makes no attempt to present an exhaustive ecclesiology; its only purpose is to present the New Testament's teaching about the local church in a practical way. More specifically, it concerns "The Love Of Christ In The Local Congregation."

A Biblical Basis

The Bible, particularly the New Testament, has much to say about various aspects of "church life." It speaks in a self-consistent and authoritative way about the local congregation, its marks of maturity, and the mutual responsibilities of its members. Its instruction comes to us in both positive and negative forms, teaching us by explicit commands and prohibitions as well as by illustrative examples. Some of the congregational situations addressed in the New Testament reveal disgraceful relationships within local Christian communities. In fact, most of the letters in the New Testament were originally written to instruct members of various local churches concerning their attitudes and actions toward one another.

The ultimate goals of this book are to teach Christians in local churches what it means to love one another with the love of Christ, and to motivate them to practice the teaching. John records a tremendously weighty commandment of Jesus, addressed primarily to the apostles, but equally applicable to those who would believe in Him through their word:

> *"A new command I give you: Love one another. As I have loved you, so you must love one another."* [1]

The newness of this commandment inheres in the standard: "as I have loved you." Had Jesus omitted this phrase, the disciples might well have said, "What's so 'new'about loving our neighbor? God taught us through Moses to love our neighbor as ourselves." [2] But the commandment to love one another is new in its loftiness and its clarity, as revealed and embodied in Jesus of Nazareth. The love we are to have for one another as disciples of Jesus is to be an "even-as-Christ-loved-us" love. [3]

The Priority Of Love

The priority of any local church must be love, because love is the basic identifying characteristic of the New Testament church. If we zero in on anything else and say, "This is what makes us different from the world around us and distinguishes us from sects and cults," we have not yet attained

---

[1] John 13:34. [2] See Lev. 19:18.
[3] See Eph. 5:1-2, 25; 1 John 3:16-18.

5

God's clearly revealed priority for His people. The identifying badge of Christian discipleship is this distinctive quality of love toward our fellow-disciples.

In the hours before Jesus' atoning death, He made a great intercession in which He vocalized His most urgent concerns to His heavenly Father. Jesus prayed:

". . . that all of them may be one, Father, just as you are in me and I am in you." [4]

Think of the oneness of the Godhead: the Father, Son, and Spirit. What kind of oneness is this? It is not a relationship of jealousy, envy, disagreement, contention, strife, bickering, and fighting among the members of the one Godhead. Rather, it is a relationship of mutual sacrifice, submission, and sharing in a common life, with a single purpose. That is the kind of unity and love we are called to have "one for another." [5]

We are immediately tempted to evade the clarity and urgency of this colossal commandment by relegating it to the realm of the idealistic or the mystical. But Jesus never discussed impractical or unattainable ideals. He refused to burden God's people with heavy loads that He Himself was unwilling or unable to bear. [6]

On the contrary, it was the very love that He had consistently demonstrated to His disciples which He now required of them. Jesus insisted that His unique love be practiced among the members of His spiritual body. When this love is

---

[4]John 17:21.   [5]See Eph. 4:1-6 and Phil. 2:1-13.
[6]See Matt. 23:1-4 and 11:28-30.

6

practiced, it will be perceived; when it is neglected, it will surely be missed. We can clearly see this concrete quality of Christ's love, not only in the example of Jesus, but also in the implication of His words: "All men will know you are my disciples if you love one another."

God's Plan For His People

The expression "one another" occurs repeatedly in the New Testament, as does the concept, "members one of another."[7] The Bible knows nothing of being a member of the body of Christ *in isolation*. It consistently speaks of Christians *in social relationship*: "members one of another." This is not to deny that, occasionally, individuals somehow hear and respond obediently to the truth of the gospel of Christ apart from the influence and ministry of a local church. Such a person would certainly be a member of the church universal, though not yet of a local congregation. But this is neither the norm nor God's plan for the development and growth of disciples of Christ.

What Do You Mean, "Church"?

Our English word "church" is translated from a compound Greek word which literally means: "a calling out of."[8] The church is that body of people whom God, by the power of the gospel of His Son, *calls out* of the moral and spiritual

---

[7] See John 13:34-35; 15:12, 17; Rom. 12:5, 16; 13:8; 14:13, 19; 15:5-7, 14; 16:16; 1 Cor. 11:33; 12:25-27; 16:20; 2 Cor. 13:12; Gal. 5:13-15, 26; 6:1-2; Eph. 4:2, 25, 32; 5:21; Phil. 2:3-4; Col. 3:9, 13; 1 Thess. 3:12; 4:9-10, 18; 5:11, 15; 2 Thess. 1:3; Heb. 3:13; 10:24-25; James 4:11; 5:9, 16; 1 Peter 1:22; 4:8-10; 5:5, 14; 1 John 1:7; 3:11, 23; 4:7, 11-12; 2 John 5.

[8] *Ekklesia*, from *ek*, out of, and *klesis*, a calling.

darkness of this world, that they might know, love, and serve Him as His own people.[9] In the New Testament, the term "church" has four applications to the people of God: universal, local, provincial, and dynamic. Although the functioning of the church at the local level is the main focus of the New Testament and of this book, a brief survey of the New Testament's usages of the term "church" will deepen our understanding of this word in all of its applications.

The Church Universal

"And I tell you that you are Peter, and on this rock I will build my church, and the gates of Hades will not overcome it." [10]

The context very plainly shows that Jesus speaks of the establishing of His church in the universal sense. He refers to His one church, the one "body of Christ" as it exists throughout the world, made up of all who respond in obedient faith to the truth of the gospel. This church also extends beyond space and time, encompassing those who have gone before us and those who are yet to come.[11] When Jesus said, "I will build my church," He spoke of the church for which He was to die, the new creation which would be established at the cost of His own blood.[12]

This prophecy was fulfilled at some point between its utter-

---

[9]See Rom. 6:1-23; 2 Cor. 6:16-18; Eph. 2:1-10; 4:17-24; Col. 1:12-14; 2 Thess. 2:13-14; 1 Peter 1:1-2; 2:9-10; Rev. 5:9-10.
[10]Matt. 16:18.
[11]See Heb. 12:22-23; Eph. 1:13-14; Rom. 8:28-30.
[12]See Acts 20:28 and 1 Peter 1:18-21.

ance by Jesus at Caesarea Philippi and the deaths of Ananias and Sapphira, for Luke's record of this latter incident contains the New Testament's first reference to "the church" as an established reality.[13] All of the available biblical evidence fixes the founding of Christ's church at the time when the sending of the Spirit of God from heaven transformed the small community of disciples into a distinctively new creation. These now believed in God through their risen Lord, and in their hearts the Spirit had firmly implanted the cry, "Abba, Father!" The apostle Peter referred to all members of this Spirit-indwelt community when he commanded Christians to "love the brotherhood,"[14] meaning "all who commonly hold to the essential Christian distinctives."[15]

The Church Local

The word "church" is applied to any *local* group of Christians who realize among themselves a covenant relationship as "members one of another." Matthew was certainly not the first New Testament writer to use "church" in its local sense, but his quotation of Jesus does preserve the first such application of the word in the New Testament:

> *"If he refuses to listen to them, tell it to the church; and if he refuses to listen even to the church, treat him as you would a pagan or a tax collector."* [16]

---

[13]See Acts 5:11. The word 'church' also occurs in Acts 2:47 in some late manuscripts and is found in the KJV.
[14]1 Peter 2:17.
[15]I know of no statement of Christian essentials more concise and complete than that of Paul in Eph. 4:4-6.
[16]Matt. 18:17.

Although Jesus spoke to His disciples in the cultural context of the Judaism of the local synagogue, Matthew has Him saying "church" (*ekklesia*) rather than "synagogue" (*sunagoge*) in this record of His teaching about disciplinary action in the local community of believers. Apparently Jesus' original statement, probably spoken in Aramaic, expressed His conviction that the true Israel of God was none other than the mixed community of believers that was following Him. They were not merely another synagogue; they were the "church" (Hebrew: *qahal*): the assembly of God's elect people. Jesus seems to have envisioned the existence of individual messianic communities, tied together by a common submission to His authority, yet each having its own local affairs to manage. The unanimous testimony of later New Testament history confirms Jesus' vision of the development of church structure.

> To the church of God in Corinth, to those sanctified in Christ Jesus and called to be holy, together with all those everywhere who call on the name of our Lord Jesus Christ—their Lord and ours....[17]

Here we see exactly that which Jesus had anticipated: numerous local congregations, all acknowledging the lordship of Jesus, with the apostle specifically addressing the church at Corinth concerning its own internal affairs.[18]

In his second treatise, which describes the early history of the Spirit-empowered church as the continuation of "all that

---

[17]1 Cor. 1:2.
[18]The authority of Christ in the local congregation, as mediated by the inspired writing of His apostles, is clearly affirmed in language which recalls the words of Jesus (see 1 Cor. 5:3-5 and compare Matt. 18:15-20).

Jesus began to do and to teach," Luke speaks of this same pattern of congregational order:

> *On that day a great persecution broke out against the church at Jerusalem, and all except the apostles were scattered throughout Judea and Samaria.*[19]

The text says the persecution here mentioned was confined to "the church at Jerusalem." God used this terrible outburst of violence against that local church to motivate the spread of Christianity into "all Judea and Samaria," as Jesus had promised.[20] The apostles, however, who originally received the Great Commission, were apparently the last members of the Jerusalem congregation to carry the faith outside the city limits!

Everything the New Testament teaches concerning the universal church *is to have visible expression and practical application in the local congregation.*[21] Obviously, the universal church must remain an abstraction until it is "made flesh," that is, manifested by means of local congregations. Paul referred to these distinct local groups as "churches of Christ."[22]

The Church Provincial

There is a *provincial* application of the term "church" in the New Testament, but its plural usage in those rare passages strongly suggests reference to the local churches within a designated province.

---

[19]Acts 8:1.   [20]See Acts 1:8.
[21]The best way to see this point is to read carefully Paul's Epistle to the Ephesians.
[22]See Rom. 16:16.

11

Now about the collection for God's people: Do what I told the Galatian churches to do.[23]

And now, brothers, we want you to know about the grace that God has given the Macedonian churches.[24]

I was personally unknown to the churches of Judea that are in Christ.[25]

Galatia, Macedonia, and Judea were not church dioceses, but rather political and cultural territories of the Roman empire in which local churches lived. Cultural distinctions may have accounted for some variation in Christian expressions and forms from province to province. Still, there was a true spiritual unity among the many first-century congregations that made them all "one church."

The Church Dynamic

The *dynamic* usage of the word "church" refers to God's people functioning as an assembled body:

In the following directives I have no praise for you, for your meetings do more harm than good. In the first place, I hear that when you come together as a church, there are divisions among you, and to some extent I believe it.[26]

The relationship of this concept to that of locally distinct groups of believers is unmistakable. Therefore, although popular misuse of the word "church" may deem inadvisable the phrase, "going to church," it is a perfectly legitimate expression—provided one has in mind the local as-

---

[23]1 Cor. 16:1.   [24]2 Cor. 8:1.   [25]Gal. 1:22.
[26]1 Cor. 11:17-18 (see also 1 Cor. 14:4-5, 12, 19, 26, 28, 34-35).

sembly of God's people, rather than a structure with stained-glass windows and a steeple.

The Church As "Family"

The Bible speaks of the church primarily as local groups of God's people—working, worshipping, and interacting with one another in a spiritual body with Christ as the Head. If we do not understand this, we have missed the life-style God intended for His people in the world. Being a member of the church is more than simply having one's name on a church roll or in a directory. Yet, such superficial understandings of "church membership" persist and prevail. Many would say in the same breath, "Yes, I'm a member of the church, and I'm also a member of the local country club." But church membership is and must be radically different from membership in any institution of human origin.

We will not understand our responsibility toward the Lord and toward one another if we miss the teaching of the Bible concerning the local congregation. The church is a living corporate entity, not a mere corporation. It is an organism, not an organization; a family, not a factory. The Bible makes it clear that *God's people need each other!* Most of us need to rethink the biblical presentation of the church as God's *family.*[27] Christians have the same Father and the same elder brother, Jesus Christ. Through adoption in Christ, we become brothers and sisters. This family concept implies family relationships and responsibilities.

Imagine visiting a family you have known for many years.

---

[27]See Matt. 12:46-50; 18:15-35; 23:8; 25:40; John 20:17; 1 Tim. 3:15; Heb. 2:11-15; 1 John 3:1-10.

Sitting down to eat with them, you suddenly notice that one of their children is missing. You ask, "Where's little Johnny? Why isn't he here?" The father replies casually, "Well, I don't know where that boy could be. He just didn't show up for dinner a couple of years ago, and none of us has heard from him since. Would you please pass the butter?" Can you imagine such cool indifference concerning an immediate family member? But is this incredible display of unconcern really unlike our own behavior sometimes in the family of God? The body of Christ is the family of God, and yet some can disappear from the midst of the family without even being missed by their own brothers and sisters.

Obviously, many Christians do not understand the importance of our relationship to one another in the local church. In the following pages, the biblical teaching concerning the nature of the local congregation and the quality of its member relationships is presented in hope of making a positive contribution toward the building up of the body of Christ.

2

THE DEFINITION AND DESCRIPTION OF THE LOCAL CHURCH

It is impossible to carry out most of the Lord's commandments to His people except in the context of relationships in a local congregation.[28] Most of the New Testament writings were addressed to local Christian communities rather than to isolated individuals, and even those few that address individuals (such as Timothy, Titus, and Philemon) speak also to congregational situations. The New Testament knows nothing of the modern phenomenon of the "floating membership" (or "members at large") in which Christians drift aimlessly into involvement with everyone in general and no one in particular. The normal Christian life-style portrayed in the New Testament involves a *decisive commitment* to a *definite community* of believers on a *day-to-day basis.*

---

[28]For example, consult a concordance for the various "one another" passages in the New Testament.

When Is It A Church?

What constitutes a local congregation, according to the New Testament? When does a group of brothers and sisters in Christ become a local church? While giving no formal reply to these questions, the New Testament nevertheless offers certain guidelines which help us to define and describe the local church. We must draw our conclusions by carefully considering all the available biblical evidence.

Obedience To The Same Gospel

The etymology of the word "church" (Greek: *ekklesia*) suggests that the local congregation is composed of those who have been "called out" of the world and into the fellowship and service of God through the gospel of Jesus Christ. All who are "members one of another" in the local church have obeyed the same gospel:

> *But we ought always to thank God for you, brothers loved by the Lord, because from the beginning God chose you to be saved through the sanctifying work of the Spirit and through belief in the truth. He called you to this through our gospel, that you might share in the glory of our Lord Jesus Christ.* [29]

Submission To The Same Lord

The local church is made up of those who have individually submitted to one another under the lordship of Jesus Christ:

> *Submit to one another out of reverence for Christ. Wives, submit to your husbands as to the Lord.... Husbands, love your*

---

[29] 2 Thess. 2:13-14. See also 1 Cor. 1:1-17; 15:1-4; Eph. 4:1-6; Col. 1:21-23.

wives, just as Christ loved the church and gave himself up for her.... Children, obey your parents in the Lord, for this is right.... Fathers, do not exasperate your children; instead, bring them up in the training and instruction of the Lord. Slaves, obey your earthly masters with respect and fear, and with sincerity of heart, just as you would obey Christ....And masters, treat your slaves in the same way. Do not threaten them, since you know that he who is both their Master and yours is in heaven, and there is no favoritism with him.[30]

Members of the local Christian community have given themselves to serve the Lord Jesus Christ and (in so doing) one another. In fact, serving the Lord's people is the same as serving the Lord Himself.[31]

Organizational Autonomy

Local churches of the New Testament were organizationally independent bodies of believers. Each congregation was a self-contained corporate unit, governed only by the Lord through His inspired Scriptures and Spirit-guided apostles and prophets. The New Testament knows nothing of modern ecclesiastical hierarchies. There is wisdom in this divine order: if ten independent (through interrelated) congregations exist within a certain province, doctrinal or ethical error will have great difficulty making headway throughout the churches, since they would have to be infected one at a time. But in a diocese concept, the ten churches could be swept away in one move because each church would be controlled by the same central governing organization. Not so in the Lord's plan for His church: each congregation was governmentally autonomous from all others, functioning independently under the lordship of

---

[30]Eph. 5:21-22, 25; 6:1,4-5, 9 (see also Rom. 14:15-19; Gal. 5:13-15).
[31]See Matt. 25:31-46; Rom. 12:1-8; 1 Peter 4:10-11.

Christ.[32] Yet, the organizational distinctiveness of each New Testament congregation was not allowed to degenerate into excessive self-concern or introversion.

A Living Organism

According to the New Testament, a local church is a group of people who are functioning as members of a living organism. Each local church member is to inject life and vitality into the body of Christ by his or her contribution of personal resources and abilities to the local congregation and its work. The life of any local congregation depends on the functioning of its members. As every joint supplies its own unique contribution and every member its own special gift, the local body is built up in love. Christians are to grow up together into the likeness of Christ.[33]

Love Is The Life-blood

Christ's Spirit animates His body (the church), and His love is its life-blood. Love (the fruit of the Spirit) indicates the presence of the Spirit. Where the Spirit is, there is life, for He is "the Spirit of life."[34] Conversely, the absence of the Spirit (evidenced by a lack of love) denotes the absence of life.

We know that we have passed from death to life, because we love our brothers. Anyone who does not love remains in death. Anyone who hates his brother is a murderer, and you know that no murderer has eternal life in him.[35]

[32]See Rev. 2:1-3:22; Acts 14:23.
[33]See Eph. 4:7-16 (compare also Rom. 12:3-8; 1 Cor. 12:12-27; 1 Peter 4:9-11).
[34]See Rom. 8:1-2; 2 Cor. 3:3-6.   [35]1 John 3:14-15.

18

Although the Spirit's fruit (singular—not "fruits") is pre-eminently love, this fruit is mult-faceted; it also encompasses joy, peace, kindness, goodness, faithfulness, gentleness, self-control, and all other such Christlike qualities.[36] The Spirit will not abundantly bring forth His fruit in us if we are constantly grieving Him by setting our minds on the flesh (self-centered concerns) instead of the Spirit (God's will in Christ).

> *Those who live according to the sinful nature [flesh] have their minds set on what that nature desires; but those who live in accordance with the Spirit have their minds set on what the Spirit desires.*[37]

> *Those who belong to Christ Jesus have crucified the sinful nature [flesh] with its passions and desires. Since we live by the Spirit, let us keep in step with the Spirit. Let us not become conceited, provoking and envying each other.*[38]

It is God's will in Christ that His people function together on the basis of love. The church is not to be an inanimate institution; it is not a mere organization. It is, according to God's purpose, a vital organism which functions and grows on the basis of love, as each member contributes its own unique gift(s), working in its own particular area for the building up of the whole body.

All For One And One For All

A local church exists where a group of people have entered into a covenant relationship of responsibility toward one another under the lordship of Christ. The individual mem-

---

[36]See Gal. 5:22-23.
[37]Rom. 8:5.   [38]Gal. 5:24-26.

ber has definite responsibility to the whole body:

*Now the body is not made up of one part but of many. If the
foot should say, "Because I am not a hand, I do not belong to
the body," it would not for that reason cease to be part of the
body. And if the ear should say, "Because I am not an eye, I
do not belong to the body," it would not for that reason cease
to be part of the body....Now you are the body of Christ, and
each one of you is a part of it.*[39]

Since the local church is made up of many individual
members and yet is one body, it naturally follows that, even
as the individual members are responsible to the whole
body, the whole body is likewise responsible for each of its
members:

*It is actually reported that there is sexual immorality among
you, and of a kind that does not occur even among pagans: A
man has his father's wife. And you are proud! Shouldn't you
rather have been filled with grief and have put out of your fellowship the man who did this?*[40]

Who was held responsible for the immoral behavior among
God's people at Corinth? The Spirit of God, through Paul,
holds the entire Corinthian congregation answerable to the
Lord Jesus for the continuation of this sin in the midst of
the local fellowship. The Spirit of Christ similarly spoke
through John to the church at Pergamum:

*"Nevertheless, I have a few things against you: You have
people there who hold to the teaching of Balaam, who taught
Balak to entice the Israelites to sin by eating food sacrificed
to idols and by committing sexual immorality. Likewise you
also have those who hold to the teaching of the Nicolaitans.*

---

[39] 1 Cor. 12:14-16, 27.
[40] 1 Cor. 5:1-2.

Repent therefore! Otherwise, I will soon come to you and will fight against them with the sword of my mouth. He who has an ear, let him hear what the Spirit says to the churches." [41]

This principle of community solidarity is prevalent throughout the Old Testament. In an extended narrative, the historian describes the sin of Achan, who stole from the spoils of Jericho certain items which were "under the ban" of destruction and devotion to Yahweh:

> *But the sons of Israel acted unfaithfully in regard to the things under the ban, for Achan... took some of the things under the ban, therefore the anger of the LORD burned against the sons of Israel.... So the LORD said to Joshua,"Rise up! Why is it that you have fallen on your face? Israel has sinned, and they have also transgressed My covenant which I commanded them. And they have even taken some of the things under the ban and have both stolen and deceived. Moreover, they have also put them among their own things. Therefore the sons of Israel cannot stand before their enemies; they turn their backs before their enemies, for they have become accursed. I will not be with you any more unless you destroy the things under the ban from your midst.... And it shall be that the one who is taken with the things under the ban shall be burned with fire, he and all that belongs to him, because he has transgressed the covenant of the LORD, and because he has committed a disgraceful thing in Israel."* [42]

Healthy Members, Healthy Body

The health of the Christian community depends on the state of its relationship to God, which in turn depends on the

---

[41]Rev. 2:14-17; see also 2:20-29.
[42]Josh. 7:1, 10-12, 15 (New American Standard Version).

spiritual health of its individual members. If a member becomes imperiled in its relationship to the Head (Christ), the body as a whole becomes imperiled in its relationship to the Head. Local churches should encourage diversity and individuality among their members, since normal bodies need many different parts. But any individualism in which members refuse to care for one another is out of place in the church. Relationship to the Head involves relationship to one's fellow body members. We cannot say that we love God while refusing to care for our brothers and sisters in Christ, for they are His children.

> *If anyone says, "I love God," yet hates his brother, he is a liar. For anyone who does not love his brother, whom he has seen, cannot love God, whom he has not seen. And He has given us this command: Whoever loves God must also love his brother. Everyone who believes that Jesus is the Christ is born of God, and everyone who loves the father loves his child as well.*[43]

The apostle leaves no doubt that he is speaking of "love" in a very personal, practical, and concrete sense, such as could be applied consistently only among a local community of believers:

> *If anyone has material possessions and sees his brother in need but has no pity on him, how can the love of God be in him? Dear children, let us not love with words or tongue but with actions and in truth.*[44]

John speaks of the same practical sensitivity among members of God's family as that which Paul enjoins upon mem-

---

[43] 1 John 4:20-5:1 (compare also 1 John 3:11-20).
[44] 1 John 3:17-18 (compare Acts 2:42-47 and 4:32-35).

bers of the body of Christ:

> —*so that there should be no division in the body, but that its parts should have equal concern for each other. If one part suffers, every part suffers with it; if one part is honored, every part rejoices with it.*[45]

Diversity should not degenerate into division, nor individuality into individualism. No man is an island in the body of Christ. The whole body is affected by the behavior of a single member. If our brother's suffering does not grieve us, if our sister's joy does not gladden our hearts, it is only because of our own ignorance and insensitivity. This is the very meaning of the "body" concept: Who hits his thumb or stubs his toe while the rest of his body remains uninformed and unconcerned about the plight of the injured member? This is Paul's point as he writes that the various parts of Christ's body "should have equal concern for each other," an inconceivable idea except on a local congregational basis. In fact, all the New Testament's "one another" teachings are virtually impossible to practice apart from the living relationships within the local congregation.

A Distinctive Community

It is imperative that the church clearly distinguish itself from the world in its beliefs, teachings, and life-style. Fellowship in the body of Christ must differ obviously and absolutely from membership in any man-made society. God always makes a distinction between those who are His

---

[45] 1 Cor. 12:25-26.

people and those who are not:

> *"But on that day I will set apart the land of Goshen, where My people are living, so that no swarms of insects will be there, in order that you may know that I, the LORD, am in the midst of the land. And I will put a division between My people and [Pharaoh's] people."* [46]

> *"I have given them your word and the world has hated them, for they are not of the world any more than I am of the world."* [47]

> *But you are a chosen people, a royal priesthood, a holy nation, a people belonging to God, that you may declare the praises of him who called you out of darkness into his wonderful light.* [48]

> *I have written you in my letter not to associate with sexually immoral people—not at all meaning the people of this world who are immoral, or the greedy and swindlers, or idolators. In that case you would have to leave this world. But now I am writing you that you must not associate with anyone who calls himself a brother but is sexually immoral or greedy, an idolator or a slanderer, a drunkard or a swindler. With such a man do not even eat. What business is it of mine to judge those outside the church? Are you not to judge those inside? God will judge those outside."Expel the wicked man from among you."* [49]

The Bible consistently affirms that Christians are "members belonging to one another," and not to the world. Local

---

[46]Exod. 8:22-23 (New American Standard Version); compare also Exod. 9:4 and 11:7.

[47]John 17:14.

[48]1 Peter 2:9 (compare also Col. 1:13-14 and Acts 26:15-18).

[49]1 Cor. 5:9-13.

church members should regard themselves as citizens of a unique society, called out of this world that they might know, love, and serve God. Each of them, having obeyed the same gospel, has been specially fitted into the body of Christ by God Himself. God's people must recapture the vision of their own distinctiveness from the world which once energized their missionary zeal and their moral excellence, but which has been all but lost through the influence of worldly thinking, religious syncretism, and indiscriminate ecumenism. The local church's teaching and life-style must be kept pure, according to biblical standards, if the Lord's people are to be the salt of the earth and the light of the world.

The Local Assembly

The local congregation, as described in the New Testament, met together on a regular basis:

> They devoted themselves to the apostles' teaching and to the fellowship, to the breaking of bread and to prayer.... All the believers were together and had everything in common.... Every day they continued to meet together in the temple courts. They broke bread in their homes and ate together with glad and sincere hearts....[50]

> On the first day of the week we came together to break bread.[51]

> In the following directives I have no praise for you, for your meetings do more harm than good. In the first place, I hear that when you come together as a church, there are divisions among you....[52]

---

[50] Acts 2:42, 44, 46.
[51] Acts 20:7.
[52] 1 Cor. 11:17-18.

*What then shall we say, brothers? When you come together,
everyone has a hymn, or a word of instruction, a revelation, a
tongue or an interpretation. All of these must be done for the
strengthening of the church.*[53]

*Now about the collection for God's people: Do what I told the
Galatian churches to do. On the first day of every week, each
one of you should set aside a sum of money in keeping with
his income, so that when I come no collections will have to be
made.*[54]

*Suppose a man comes into your meeting wearing a gold ring
and fine clothes, and a poor man in shabby clothes also comes
in.*[55]

*Let us not give up meeting together, as some are in the habit
of doing, but let us encourage one another....*[56]

Apparently, the church at Jerusalem immediately began to
meet on a daily basis for instruction, encouragement,
prayer, and mutual interaction, although this practice of
daily meetings was not necessarily imitated in other local
churches. Local church members met together regularly to
recall the Lord's death in the breaking of bread, as Jesus
had commanded. The Lord's Supper was the visible sign of
the covenant relationship between the Lord and His people.
The covenant meal re-told the story of the central event
which bound the church to the Lord of the covenant and to
one another: the passion (and resurrection) of Christ. According to both biblical and non-biblical sources, Christians
customarily met together as local churches on the first day
of each week to edify one another and honor the Lord in the

---

[53] 1 Cor. 14:26. [54] 1 Cor. 16:1-2.
[55] James 2:2. [56] Heb. 10:25.

26

sharing of the Supper. The first day of the week, being that day of the week on which Jesus rose from the dead, had become known in Christian circles as "the Lord's Day" by the time John wrote the Revelation.[57] Undoubtedly, there were also other, less formal gatherings for worship and fellowship among the local churches.

Freedom And Unity In Christ

Present-day local churches practice many traditions and customs that were not found among the first-century churches. Nevertheless, some of these practices are allowable and desirable. The New Testament records nothing about "church buildings." Rather, it speaks of Christians meeting together in the temple at Jerusalem and in homes. The cultural situation in which the church was born made these the most appropriate forms to use. But this fact does not prohibit churches today from using other types of meeting places. The *forms* by which the church functions can (indeed, *must*) change from time to time and place to place, as the church's cultural environment changes. The Lord of the church, having commissioned His people to preach an eternal and universal gospel, gives them much liberty in this matter of adapting temporal forms to changing cultures. Those groups within Christendom which have failed to understand this balance of form and freedom have become culturally irrelevant and introverted: mere historical curiosities. Certainly, there are commandments which must be carried out regardless of the cultural environment; every-

---

[57]See Rev. 1:10.

thing is not "up for grabs." But we must carefully distinguish between *commandments* and the traditional or expedient *forms* by which to carry out the commandments. If we fail to recognize this distinction, we will pay the price of evangelistic ineffectiveness and perhaps even scandalous, unnecessary division of the body of Christ.

For example, first-century Christians obeyed the divine commandment of periodically meeting together to worship the Lord and edify one another. (Recall that much of the apostolic instruction to the church involved "one another" relationships that could only be carried out in the face-to-face interaction of a local church situation.) Granting that the New Testament's authority over the church has not waned, contemporary congregations must yet ask, "How often should we meet together?" Aside from the possibility that the practice of assembling to share the Lord's Supper on each first day of the week represents a response to an apostolic commandment, the Scriptures are silent concerning this question. Thus, we are free before the Lord, as distinct local churches, to make wise and responsible decisions regarding the frequency of our assemblies. Again, someone might ask, "What should be the structure or format of the local church's assembly?" The New Testament, aside from certain broad guidelines and examples, leaves the matter open. What time of day should the church meet together? How much time should the church spend in formal assembly? How many songs should precede the first public prayer of the assembly? Should a sermon precede or follow the sharing of the Lord's Supper? The Lord gives no command in the New Testament concerning any of these matters.

Ecclesiastical Culture Shock

Many Christians experience what could be called "ecclesiastical culture shock" when they leave their home congregations, where they have served the Lord for many years, and begin to experience life in other congregations, perhaps in other parts of the world. They have grown accustomed to certain traditional forms in their obedience to the Lord's commands to His church, and that is fine. But when these Christians see other congregations doing the same things that they have been doing at home, although under different external forms, they are often incapable of seeing beneath those forms to find the underlying common bond of faith and practice. We must refuse to permit differences in external forms to obscure our perception of the unity that exists among all those churches which are responding in truth to the same Head: the Lord Jesus Christ, who speaks through the New Testament.

As a missionary in New Zealand, I was graciously enabled to meet the challenge of acting on these principles of unity and fellowship. In that culture, it was common practice for our local churches to spend thirty minutes or more of the assembly period in the celebration of the Lord's Supper. And we were not just standing around; we had a lot to say about the occasion and its meaning. But this obviously did not mean that those churches in other cultures which spent ten or fifteen minutes sharing the Supper were "unscriptural" or wrong. The custom of the New Zealand churches is certainly one way to order a local church's assembly period, but it is not the only way.

A certain local church of which I was once a member had

decided to change their longstanding tradition of passing the contribution plate immediately after the serving of the Lord's Supper. For a number of practical reasons, the leadership believed that the interests of that particular church would best be served by taking the collection at the conclusion of the assembly period. This change was not made for the sake of novelty or innovation; it was a carefully considered decision. Nevertheless, someone wondered about it: "Wait a minute—this may not be scriptural!" Of course, we should ask ourselves whether any proposed congregational action would promote the doing of God's revealed will, or would in fact contradict it. We should thank God for those who are so conscientiously concerned to honor the Lord's will. But a clear understanding of the difference between forms and authoritative commands must be gained.

Tradition: Right Or Wrong?

Tradition is a powerful force. Jesus sternly warned against its misuse:

> *Then some Pharisees and teachers of the law came to Jesus from Jerusalem and asked, "Why do your disciples break the tradition of the elders? They don't wash their hands before they eat!" Jesus replied, "And why do you break the command of God for the sake of your tradition?...You hypocrites! Isaiah was right when he prophesied about you: These people honor me with their lips, but their hearts are far from me. They worship me in vain; their teachings are but rules taught by men."* [58]

But how different is the tone of Paul concerning tradition:

---

[58]Matt 15:1-3, 7-9.

*So then, brothers, stand firm and hold to the teachings [liter-
ally, traditions] we passed on to you, whether by word of
mouth or by letter.*[59]

Obviously, tradition, as such, is neither right nor wrong.
Nor is the source of a given tradition necessarily the decisive factor in determining its value, for beneficial traditions
can come from either God or man. But it is always spiritually destructive to elevate a non-authoritative, non-biblical
tradition to the status of a divine commandment, and then to
bind it on others. It is as wrong to bind non-authoritative
traditions on others as it is to ignore the authority of clear
biblical commands.

We should not be surprised to find brothers and sisters in
Christ who are doing the same things in their local churches
that we are doing in ours, but in forms that differ, even radically, from our own. Churches are not locked in to only
one or two ways of evangelizing, of teaching God's Word,
of building up one another in the faith. Our options are not
limited to "the way that we've always done it before." The
local church should consider every means of building up its
members and reaching out to the lost with the gospel; those
which are most effective in carrying out the Lord's will
should be implemented. Let us throw off the shackles of
counterproductive, non-authoritative traditions that only
hinder our individual and collective growth as members of
Christ's body.

Let Love Rule

As congregations consider various forms through which to

[59]2 Thess. 2:15.

31

obey the Lord's commands, the love of Christ must be the final arbitrator. The changing of established methods and forms, even for the best of reasons, can be a traumatic experience for those who have become comfortable and secure in their traditions. What should be done when a local church member wants his congregation to reconsider the forms in which it is expressing its "body life"? Should our trailblazing brother stand up one morning in the midst of the local assembly, and shout and stomp his feet until he manipulates the church into making the desired adjustments? We must confess that scenes such as this are all too familiar in certain local churches.

No doubt, the Lord's provision of pastors (elders) to tend the members and oversee the work of the local congregation will help in resolving such problems for those churches which are blessed with qualified leadership. The local church's final answer to differences of opinion concerning its external forms is not the mere presence of a leadership structure, however. A sensitivity of body members toward one another and the speaking of truth in love to one another are the only solutions which are more than temporary and superficial. The love of Christ in the local congregation will move members to talk to one another candidly, sincerely, and constructively. Wise elders will always seek out feedback from members of the local church in making decisions regarding the local church's forms and methods of doing the Lord's will. They will consider the needs and abilities of all the local members whom they serve, and they will resist the temptation to exercise authority which belongs only to the Lord. Godly elders will remember that they are overseeing and tending a flock that is not their own.

Qualified local church leadership is a wonderful gift from

God; it is His plan and provision for the well-being of His people and the ongoing of His purpose in Christ. But God has given something to the church that is even more essential to congregational life than qualified elders : *the love of Christ!* The local church needs love, joy, peace, patience, kindness, goodness, faithfulness, gentleness, and self control among its members as they interact with one another. The fruit of the Spirit does not grow in a vacuum; these are relating-to-one-another qualities that define what it means to "love even as Christ loved." May God help us to grow together in the love of Christ, into a genuine willingness to lay down our lives for one another.

3

BALANCE AND THE BODY CONCEPT IN THE LOCAL CHURCH

In chapter two, the idea of a "balance" between form and freedom was introduced: There must be *structure* in the local church in order for it to respond to the authority of its Lord, but there must also be *freedom* for each local church to adapt its forms to the cultural environment in which it exists. This concept of balance will serve as a springboard into further consideration of the work and internal life of the local congregation.

A Package Deal

The local congregation is the only unit of organization known to the writers of the New Testament in which the Lord's revealed will for His people is to be fulfilled. Still, there are always those "pioneer spirits" who consider themselves spiritually self-sufficient as regards the church: "I can do it all by myself. I don't need anybody else. My relationship to the Lord has absolutely nothing to do with my relationship to members of the church." Nothing could be further from the truth:

> *And God placed all things under his* [Jesus'] *feet and appointed him to be head over everything for the church, which is his body, the fullness of him who fills everything in every way.*[60]

Although this passage speaks of the church in the universal sense, the point remains: the church is Christ's "fullness." Most interpreters take this to mean that the church, as Christ's body, is that which "fills," or completes, Christ Himself in the eternal purpose and plan of God. To be related to Christ is to be related to His body, and, as has been noted, everything Paul has to say concerning the church universal is to be visibly and practically expressed in the local congregation. Christ and the church are a "package deal"; in order to have one, you must also take the other. He is the Head, the church is His body.

Where does the New Testament locate the responsibility of disciples to be "members belonging to one another"? In what situation does there need to be qualified Christians to serve as elders, deacons, Bible teachers, givers, helpers, evangelists, and so on? What is the context in which the principle of corrective disciplinary action must be carried out in order to preserve and promote purity among disciples of Christ? The answer, in each case, is "the local congregation." We are driven to the conclusion that God has designed the local congregation (and *only* the local congregation, however large or small it may be) to carry out the

---

[60]Eph. 1:22-23 (compare also Acts 9:1-5 and Col. 1:24).

work that Jesus and His apostles have commanded His people to do. In order to be a truly functioning member of the body of Christ, each Christian must be actively involved as a member of a local congregation.

Building Up And Reaching Out

The work of the church (the Lord's will for His people, as revealed in Scripture) can be summarized under two categories: edification and evangelism. There is to be a simultaneous function of the body *building itself up* in love, as it *reaches out* to the lost. An unbalanced congregation is one which has a strong evangelistic thrust, but little or no edification of its own members. Souls are being brought in, but the body is weak and undernourished; it cannot sustain the new members, and so eventually they die. On the other hand, imbalance exists in any local church in which the members have resolved only to edify themselves, and to let the lost remain lost. Every local church needs a balanced approach to its own work if it is to do the Lord's will.

Restoring The Letter And The Spirit

Many people are concerned with the restoration of the Christianity about which we read in the New Testament. Customarily, the approach to restoration has been to recover the mechanics, the externals of the early church: a restoration of biblical practice concerning church organization and congregational autonomy, the elements of worship, and such things as these. Certainly, these things are important, but if Jesus were to comment on our efforts, He would probably say something like this:

"But you have neglected the more important matters.... You should have practiced the latter, without neglecting the former." [61]

Paul also would probably be inclined to show us a "more excellent way."

This matter of balance is crucial. If we restore the letter but ignore the spirit of New Testament Christianity, we have become only a resounding gong or a clanging cymbal. A church without love is a dead church, a lifeless body. A congregation that is not distinguished primarily by members loving one another will soon cease to be a New Testament church, if it has not already lost its identity. We insist on hanging up a sign to tell the world that "The Church Of Christ Meets Here," but Jesus refuses to let it go at that:

"All men will know that you are my disciples if you love one another." [62]

The Corinthian church lacked no spiritual gift; yet that congregation was being destroyed from within by various divisions and disorders. Christians were exalting themselves over each other, despising each other, permitting sin to destroy each other, and even suing each other before unbelievers. They had every gift, but yet they lacked one essential quality, the love of Christ, which is the life-blood of the local congregation, and the measure of its maturity. A local church may have a tremendously gifted membership; it may enjoy all kinds of wonderful programs and dynamic ministries. It can be a buzzing hive of activity, its assemblies

---

[61]Matt. 23:23.
[62]John 13:35.

filled to standing room only, week after week. But this does not necessarily mean that a congregation is mature. In fact, these things alone, as desirable as they may be, do not even assure that a congregation is *alive:*

> *"I know your deeds; you have a reputation of being alive, but you are dead."* [63]

So spoke the risen Christ to a first-century church at Sardis, and so speaks the Spirit to many congregations today. The blazing eyes of the risen Lord can see through any facade.

Meeting And Maturing

God ordained the existence and the assemblies of local congregations so that members of the body of Christ could help one another to mature into the image of Jesus Christ by showing the love of Christ to one another. This implies that local churches must have occasions of meeting together so that members can interact with one another and thus build up one another toward the goal of spiritual maturity. If Christians do not meet together, they cannot build up one another:

> *And let us consider how we may spur one another on toward love and good deeds. Let us not give up meeting together....* [64]

It is no mere coincidence that the goal of this interaction is the provocation and cultivation of "love" and "good deeds" in one another, for these very qualities summarize the life of Jesus. The measure of maturity, therefore, is the conformity of the congregation (as a collective body and as indi-

---

[63]Rev. 3:1.   [64]Heb. 10:24-25.

38

vidual members) to the character of Christ:

> —*until we all reach unity in the faith and in the knowledge of the Son of God and become mature, attaining to the whole measure of the fullness of Christ. Then we will no longer be infants, tossed back and forth by the waves.... Instead, speaking the truth in love, we will in all things grow up into him who is the Head, that is, Christ.*[65]

In order for Christians to build up one another, they must come together and *speak* to one another in truth and love. The importance of balance is seen once again: Some people want to speak in "love," but would rather forget about this business of "truth." But Paul wrote that Christians are to *speak the truth in love.* Truth is very important; we do not want to lose our balance here by saying, "I will concern myself with love, and forget about truth." There is a certain thing that is called "truth" in the Bible and we need to be concerned about it. We are called by the Father to worship "in spirit and truth."[66] The doctrinal content of our worship ("truth") is half of the picture; the attitude of our hearts ("spirit") is the other half. The spirit of our worship to God should be one of *love for one another*, since we are His children in Christ.[67]

The assembling of the local church is not simply for the purpose of going through a ritual or religious exercise. If our mental attitude toward the assembly of the local church is ritualistic, then we will derive only a ritual from the assembly. The coming together of the local church as a body is for the purpose of members building up one another. Each individual member has a contribution to make to the

---

[65]Eph. 4:13-15.
[66]See John 4:23-24.
[67]See Matt. 5:21-24; Rom. 14:17-21; 1 John 4:20-21.

spiritual growth of the rest of the members whenever the members meet together. And this "meeting together to build up one another" can be done in many ways. It is a mistake for a congregation to center its entire life as a local body on the weekly assembly of the whole church. There are many forms and opportunities in which members may interact in smaller groups and in different ways during the entire week. Let us avoid the extreme of making the Sunday morning assembly the totality of Christian living. At the same time, let us also resist the opposite danger of contributing little or nothing to the whole church as an assembled body.

The Corporate Concept

The local congregation is a corporate entity designed by God Himself. It is the people of God who, by mutual agreement, *come together* for corporate action. Our English term "corporate" is derived from the Latin word *corpus*, meaning "body." The church is to function according to a *corporate* concept; it is to act as a collective whole, as a body or an organism. Thus, Paul addresses the local church at Corinth with these words concerning their corporate responsibility toward a sinning member in their midst:

> *When you are assembled in the name of our Lord Jesus and I am with you in spirit, and the power of our Lord Jesus is present, hand this man over to Satan, so that the sinful nature may be destroyed and his spirit saved on the day of the Lord.*[68]

The purpose of this drastic measure was to motivate the sin-

---

[68] 1 Cor. 5:4-5. These words are strongly reminiscent of the instruction of Jesus concerning discipline within the community of believers (see Matt. 18:17-20).

40

ning brother to repent, so that he might ultimately be *saved*. There had to be a demonstration on earth of that which was already done in heaven: the disfellowshipping of an unrepentant, rebellious sinner. To have allowed him to continue unreproached in the midst of God's people would have been the most unloving course of action possible in that situation. To love one another "even as Christ has loved us" means that we will do whatever is necessary, go to whatever length is required, in order to help one another toward purity, holiness, and ultimate salvation in the body of Christ:

> *Here is a trustworthy saying that deserves full acceptance: Christ Jesus came into the world to save sinners....*[69]
>
> *Husbands, love your wives, just as Christ loved the church and gave himself up for her to make her holy...and to present her to himself as a radiant church, without stain or wrinkle or any other blemish, but holy and blameless.*[70]

Jesus manifested His love in this world by giving up His life to save sinners and to make God's people holy. The church, as the "new incarnation" of Christ—His body on the earth today—must also be about the business of proclaiming salvation to the lost and promoting holiness among the saved. The example and pattern of Jesus Christ has made it clear that this great work cannot be accomplished apart from a willingness to pour out one's life in the process.

---

[69]1 Tim. 1:15.   [70]Eph. 5:25-27.

4

BIBLICAL LOVE AND 'BECOMING' IN THE LOCAL CHURCH

Then we will no longer be like children, forever changing our minds about what we believe because someone has told us something different, or has cleverly lied to us and made the lie sound like the truth. Instead, we will lovingly follow the truth at all times—speaking truly, dealing truly, living truly— and so become more and more in every way like Christ who is the Head of His body, the church. Under His direction the whole body is fitted together perfectly, and each part in its own special way helps the other parts, so that the whole body is healthy and growing and full of love.[71]

To anyone who has seriously considered the teaching of Christ, particularly as summarized in the Sermon on the Mount, the concept of "becoming" is quite familiar. Jesus spoke repeatedly about the necessity of our *becoming* like Himself, that we might do the things that He embodied and commanded. No one can consistently and wholeheartedly do that which is foreign to his or her nature. This does not mean, of course, that disciples must enjoy doing all that is

---

[71]Eph. 4:14-16, *The Living Bible: Paraphrased* (Wheaton, IL: Tyndale House Publ., 1971).

42

commanded of them; it does mean that they will desire, above all things, to please the Lord who bought them at the cost of His own blood.

Discipleship And Denial Of Self

Jesus spoke about the absolute necessity of the denial of self in being His disciple:

> *Then he said to them all: "If anyone would come after me, he must deny himself and take up his cross daily and follow me. For whoever wants to save his life will lose it, but whoever loses his life for me will save it. What good is it for a man to gain the whole world, and yet lose or forfeit his very self?"* [72]

In considering this matter of becoming "conformed to the image of Christ," we should think not only of Jesus' words, but of His example in denial of self:

> *For you know the grace of our Lord Jesus Christ, that though he was rich, yet for your sakes he became poor, so that you through his poverty might become rich.* [73]

> *Your attitude should be the same as that of Christ Jesus: Who, being in very nature God, did not consider equality with God something to be grasped, but made himself nothing, taking the very nature of a servant, being made in human likeness. And being found in appearance as a man, he humbled himself and became obedient to death—even death on a cross!* [74]

> *"Abba, Father," he said, "everything is possible for you. Take this cup from me. Yet not what I will, but what you will."* [75]

---

[72]Luke 9:23-25 (see also Matt. 10:37-39; 16:24-26; Mark 8:34-37; Luke 14:25-35; John 12:25-26).
[73]2 Cor. 8:9.   [74]Phil. 2:5-8.   [75]Mark 14:36.

43

Paul also spoke clearly about the necessity of putting to death (crucifying) the "old man" and his deeds, that we might become a "new creation in Christ" and "walk in newness of life":

> *We were therefore buried with him through baptism into death in order that, just as Christ was raised from the dead through the glory of the Father, we too may live a new life.*[76]

> *Therefore, if anyone is in Christ, he is a new creation; the old has gone, the new has come!*[77]

> *I have been crucified with Christ, and I no longer live, but Christ lives in me.*[78]

> *And God raised us up with Christ and seated us with him in the heavenly realms in Christ Jesus....*[79]

> *For to me, to live is Christ....*[80]

> *...Christ in you, the hope of glory.*[81]

The purpose of refusing to permit self and its desires to reign in our lives is that we might "lovingly follow the truth at all times—speaking truly, dealing truly, living truly—and so become more and more in every way like Christ who is the Head of His body, the church." But it is not the will or purpose of God that we should grow up to mature Christlikeness as separate entities, isolated from one another:

> *Instead, speaking the truth in love, we will in all things grow up into him who is the Head, that is, Christ. From him the whole body, joined and held together by every supporting ligament, grows and builds itself up in love, as each part does its work.*[82]

---

[76]Rom. 6:4.   [77]2 Cor. 5:17.   [78]Gal. 2:20.
[79]Eph. 2:6.   [80]Phil. 1:21.   [81]Col. 1:27.   [82]Eph. 4:15-16.

A Whole New Approach

In the purpose of God, Christians are to grow together into the likeness of Christ. As members of one body, belonging to the same Head and therefore to one another, disciples of Jesus should work cooperatively together toward maturity.

This means nothing less than a revolutionary approach to life, a repudiation of that which we knew outside of Christ. Outside of Christ, our lives were characterized by the maxim, "Every man for himself." In Christ, each member belongs to every other member; the individual is equipped by God to serve the Lord by meeting the needs of the other members of the body of Christ:

> *Therefore, I urge you, brothers, in view of God's mercy, to offer your bodies as living sacrifices, holy and pleasing to God which is your spiritual worship....For by the grace given me I say to every one of you: Do not think of yourself more highly than you ought, but rather think of yourself with sober judgment, in accordance with the measure of faith God has given you. Just as each of us has one body with many members, and these members do not all have the same function, so in Christ we who are many form one body, and each member belongs to all the others. We have different gifts, according to the grace given us. If a man's gift is prophesying, let him use it in proportion to his faith. If it is serving, let him serve; if it is teaching, let him teach; if it is encouraging, let him encourage; if it is contributing to the needs of others, let him give generously; if it is leadership, let him govern diligently; if it is showing mercy, let him do it cheerfully.*[83]

> *Each one should use whatever gift he has received to serve others, faithfully administering God's grace in its various*

[83]Rom. 12:1, 3-8.

forms. If anyone serves, he should do it with the strength God provides, so that in all things God may be praised through Jesus Christ.[84]

Some Christians tend to belittle their own value and importance to the proper functioning of the body of Christ. "I'm not much," they say. "I have so little to give." But to such self-depreciation, the Spirit of God replies, "You are vitally important. You are a part of the body. The body needs you."

But in fact God has arranged the parts in the body, every one of them, just as he wanted them to be. If they were all one part, where would the body be? As it is, there are many parts, but one body. The eye cannot say to the hand, "I don't need you!" And the head cannot say to the feet, "I don't need you!" On the contrary, those parts of the body that seem to be weaker are indispensable, and the parts that we think are less honorable we treat with special honor. And the parts that are unpresentable are treated with special modesty, while our presentable parts need no special treatment.

But God has combined the members of the body and has given greater honor to the parts that lacked it, so that there should be no division in the body, but that its parts should have equal concern for each other. If one part suffers, every part suffers with it; if one part is honored, every part rejoices with it. Now you are the body of Christ, and each one of you is a part of it.[85]

Each member is a part of something eternal in both design and duration: the body of Christ! No member is what he or she is by accident. The doctrine of the priesthood of all be-

---

[84]1 Peter 4:10-11.
[85]1 Cor. 12:18-27.

lievers teaches that each Christian can acceptably serve God only by submission to Jesus Christ, and that no Christian can serve Jesus Christ without ministering to His body. Even as the Father points toward His Son, saying, "Listen to him,"[86] the Son turns to us and says, "I tell you the truth, whatever you did for one of the least of these brothers of mine, you did for me."[87] If you are a member of the body, you have to function as a part. To despise oneself or one's place in the body is to dishonor the Head of the body and the God who placed the members in the body according to His own infinite wisdom and will.

The New Corinthianism

We are not all the same in the body of Christ, regarding talents and abilities. There is a sense in which each member is a specialist, contributing his or her own unique and personal ministry to the building up of the whole body. That is why it is important for each member to remember that the Lord is concerned about the development of the whole congregation. We must avoid clannishness and cliques in the body of Christ; we must beware of the tendency to exalt one's own gift or exclusive group over the rest of the body.

In the first-century Corinthian church, there were some who boasted of their association with the "big names in the brotherhood"—Paul, Apollos, Cephas, and even a perverse exclusivism concerning the usage of the name of Christ.[88] There was also a movement within the church to elevate the status of tongue-speaking above all other gifts. I have seen this Corinthian spirit among modern churches of Christ. I

---

[86]Mark 9:7.   [87]Matt. 25:40.   [88]See 1 Cor. 1:10-13.

have witnessed the spectacle of the different programs and ministries within one local congregation competing with one another instead of rejoicing in one another's contributions to the whole body. The bus ministry competes with the visitation program. The education program tries to outshine the pulpit ministry. Sometimes members even work against one another within the same program or ministry. The vision of the whole body becomes clouded by the delusion that the church exists only for the sake of one's own personal ministry. A divisive situation develops. How can these destructive tendencies be avoided? What will enable us to realize, and to rejoice in, the truth that the development of the whole congregation hinges upon every member's good work of faith and labor of love?

Love Is The Answer

Paul wrote that the body of Christ "grows and builds itself up in love, as each part does its work." Love —the very love of Christ— is both the goal and the means to attaining the goal of maturity in the local church. Love will motivate the members of the body to set aside selfish desires and to give of themselves for the sake of the whole body. The love of Christ is the only force powerful enough to vanquish laziness, pride, selfish competitiveness, and hostility within the body of Christ. Biblical love is not a vague or shadowy "something." In a word, the most comprehensive definition of biblical love is "Christlikeness." The highest, noblest love on earth consists of Christlike attitudes and actions.

Modern psychology is finally discovering a tremendous

principle which God has long since revealed to His people: the relationship between attitudes (the inward life) and actions (the outward life). If our attitudes are negative, our actions will also be negative, for "from [the heart] flow the springs of life."[89] The keynote in the teaching of Jesus concerning true "righteousness" is its origin and motivation in the heart of the individual:

"You have heard that it was said, 'Do not commit adultery.' But I tell you that anyone who looks at a woman lustfully has already committed adultery with her in his heart."[90]

"Don't you see that whatever enters the mouth goes into the stomach and then out of the body? But the things that come out of the mouth come from the heart, and these make a man 'unclean.' For out of the heart come evil thoughts, murder, adultery, sexual immorality, theft, false testimony, slander. These are what make a man 'unclean'...."[91]

Christianity, Godliness, And Love

Christianity, then, is a matter of having our hearts "right with God." Christ is the embodiment of God, and God is love. We should never think of God as being one thing in character, and Christ as being something else. Love summarizes the character of God as He has been revealed in the historical Christ, and love is that which brings about greater likeness to Christ. A mature congregation is one in which members are loving one another with the love of Christ; they are serving one another according to the gifts and needs that exist within the body, in order to promote greater

---

[89]Prov. 4:23 (New American Standard Version).
[90]Matt. 5:27-28.
[91]Matt. 15:17-20.

closeness and conformity to Christ in each member.

The reader will have noticed a careful effort in this section to emphasize the distinctiveness of biblical love. Many myths and much misinformation darken modern society's understanding of this word "love," and it is easy to understand why this is so. The very essence of "worldliness" lies in this willful ignorance of the light of God's love:

> *"This is the verdict: Light has come into the world, but men loved darkness instead of light because their deeds were evil."* [92]

> *At one time we too were foolish, disobedient, deceived and enslaved by all kinds of passions and pleasures. We lived in malice and envy, being hated and hating one another. But when the kindness and love of God our Savior appeared, he saved us....* [93]

In modern American culture, many people rely almost exclusively on television to give them true knowledge and information. The worldly concept of love popularized by television usually has to do with an individual's self-centered intensity of emotion, secret romantic involvement, or illicit sexual experience with another person. Biblical love has an altogether different source, center, motivation, and goal:

> *This is how we know what love is: Jesus Christ laid down His life for us. And we ought to lay down our lives for our brothers.* [94]

> *Dear friends, let us love one another, for love comes from God. Everyone who loves has been born of God and knows*

---

[92]John 3:19 (see also 2 Cor. 4:3-6).
[93]Titus 3:3-4 (see also Eph. 4:17-20ff).
[94]1 John 3:16.

God. Whoever does not love does not know God, because God is love. This is how God showed his love among us: He sent his one and only Son into the world that we might live through him. This is love: not that we loved God, but that he loved us and sent his Son as an atoning sacrifice for our sins. Dear friends, since God so loved us, we also ought to love one another.[95]

Divine love, fully manifested in Christ, is a commanded love. When John writes that Christians "ought" to love one another, he is not simply making a helpful suggestion; he is showing that those who have received this divine love have a moral obligation to share it with their fellow-believers. The kind of love that is under consideration here has been commanded by God in no uncertain terms:

We know that we have passed from death to life, because we love our brothers. Anyone who does not love remains in death.[96]

And he has given us this command: Whoever loves God must also love his brother.[97]

It does not matter why a Christian might refuse to love another Christian: If there is no love, there is no life, no fellowship with God. This "love" is not based on how one person may feel toward another; yet, there is to be a development of genuine affection as this commanded love is expressed. The Holy Spirit refuses to let us remain contented with just mechanically "obeying God" in this matter of loving one another. It must begin with love for God, and it must be based on a loving response to God's commandment; but God desires that we really like one another, in the

---

[95] 1 John 4:7-11.   [96] 1 John 3:14.   [97] 1 John 4:21.

51

midst of our loving one another:

> *Be devoted to one another in brotherly love. Honor one another above yourselves.*[98]

Emotions cannot be turned off and on at will. Our emotional responses depend upon our perception of people and situations. God does not command us to instantly pump up certain emotions toward one another, and then to behave on the basis of these emotions. Instead, He expects us to respond to His love by serving one another ("as I have loved you"), and by cultivating a "brotherly" way of seeing one another and dealing with one another. As we invest more of ourselves in one another's lives, the feelings of affection will naturally come forth:

> *"For where your treasure is, there your heart will be also."*[99]

A Closer Look At Love

Let us look still more closely at the biblical concept, "the love of Christ." The Greek word characteristically used to designate the love of Christians for one another is the same one which serves to identify God's love for the world:

> *"For God so loved the world that he gave his one and only Son, that whoever believes in him shall not perish but have eternal life."*[100]

---

[98]Rom. 12:10 (compare also 1 Peter 1:22 and 2 Peter 1:7 in the Greek text).   [99]Matt. 6:21.
[100]John 3:16. The verb form of *agapao* is used here. The noun form is *agape*.

This is a kind of "love" that can be, and is, commanded. It is primarily a matter of will, intent, and purpose rather than of emotion, although emotion is not uninvolved. But there was nothing "lovable" about the world that God "so loved." The cause of this love did not reside in the nature or the response of its object: "the world" hates the light (Christ) because its deeds are evil. This love of God in Christ is an initiating love, a love that reaches out. It is a love that renounces personal rights and is not ashamed to take the first step toward establishing or strengthening a relationship. This love flows from but one fountainhead: the heart of the eternal and almighty God, who is love. Because God is who He is, He reached out in Christ and loved the unlovable. He has planted the seed of His own loving nature in each of His children:

> *Now that you have purified yourselves by obeying the truth so that you have sincere love for your brothers, love one another deeply, from the heart. For you have been born again, not of perishable seed, but of imperishable, through the living and enduring word of God....And this is the word that was preached to you.*[101]

> *See that what you have heard from the beginning remains in you....As for you, the anointing you received from him remains in you, and you do not need anyone to teach you....No one who is born of God will continue to sin, because God's seed remains in him; he cannot go on sinning, because he has been born of God. This is how we know who the children of God are and who the children of the devil are: Anyone who does not do what is right is not a child of God; neither is anyone who does not love his brother. This is the message you heard from the beginning: We should love one another.*[102]

---

[101]1 Peter 1:22-23.
[102]1 John 2:24, 27; 3:9-11.

53

God has poured out his love into our hearts by the Holy Spirit, whom he has given us.[103]

Now about brotherly love we do not need to write to you, for you yourselves have been taught by God to love each other.[104]

For all that we may hear about "Petrine," "Johannine," and "Pauline" theology, at least this much is clear: Peter, John, and Paul shared an identical view of basic Christianity. God imparts His life and His Spirit to His children through the gospel, and that gospel teaches us to love one another: "We love because he first loved us."[105]

Within the eternal Godhead it has always been, "like Father, like Son." And within God's eternal purpose to create an extended family through adoption in Christ, the same principle holds true. The brothers and sisters of Jesus must become like their elder Brother, who is Himself "the radiance of God's glory and the exact representation of his being."[106] The true test of our relationship to God (as His children) and to one another (as brothers and sisters in Christ) is this unconditional, initiating, sacrificial, laying-one's-life-down love for one another. If our generation is ever to really understand the love of God for unlovable and rebellious mankind, that love must again become incarnate through the local body of Christ. Local congregations exist so that we may love one another. In so doing, we shall help one another to grow up into "the whole measure of the fullness of Christ." We were born (again) to love. We can love. We must love.

---

[103]Rom. 5:5. [104]1 Thess. 4:9. [105]1 John 4:19. [106]Heb. 1:3.

5

THE PRACTICAL IMPACT OF LOVE IN THE LOCAL CHURCH

Love is so patient and so kind; love never boils with jealousy; it never boasts, is never puffed with pride; it does not act with rudeness, or insist upon its rights. It never gets provoked; it never harbors evil thoughts; is never glad when wrong is done, but always glad when truth prevails; it bears up under anything, it exercises faith in everything, it keeps up hope in everything, it gives us power to endure in anything. Love never fails.[107]

Reading familiar biblical passages from different translations can be a refreshing and enlightening exercise. People tend to become apathetic and indifferent toward the familiar, the habitual, and the commonplace. This principle is no less valid in the case of the teacher who is trying to communicate spiritual truth than it is in the case of the

---

[107]1 Cor. 13:1-8 (Charles B. Williams, *The New Testament in the Language of the People* [Boston: Bruce Humphries, Inc., 1937]).

homemaker who is always searching for a new tuna fish recipe. Both occupations face the challenge of stirring up slumbering taste buds by seeking out fresh approaches to the familiar. Yet, it is one of the deepest paradoxes of the kingdom of God that the simplest truths are also the most profound, that the most familiar and ordinary elements are also the most glorious. The incarnation of Christ teaches us nothing if it does not teach us this.

Accept No Substitutes!

The concept of "love" is something that is so basic and vital to the spiritual health of Christians, both individually and collectively in local churches, that we dare not forsake it in favor of any other nutrient, no matter how exotic or spicy. The tendency of some Christians to place "knowledge" above the priority of love is well documented and forcefully corrected in several New Testament texts.[108] Spiritual gifts have also been brought into competition for main dish on the Christian menu. The Spirit of God does not despise knowledge or gifts; indeed, all such virtues and blessings proceed from Him. Nevertheless, the apostle tells us that, whereas revealed knowledge and supernatural gifts were to cease, the church will never outgrow its need for the sustenance of faith, hope, and love:

> *Love never fails. But where there are prophecies, they will cease; where there are tongues, they will be stilled; where there is knowledge, it will pass away....And now these three remain: faith, hope and love. But the greatest of these is love.*[109]

---

[108]See especially 1 John and Paul's epistles to the Corinthians and the Colossians.   [109]1 Cor. 13:8, 13.

"But the greatest of these is love." Almost instinctively we ask, "Why? What is so great about 'love'?" Faith is (in one sense) more basic, more foundational to Christian experience than is love. Everything is built upon faith.[110] There can be neither hope nor love without faith. Yet, Paul says that love is the greatest blessing that God has bestowed upon the church, and the greatest responsibility that He has entrusted to her. To understand why this is so, we must first consider the practical impact that love can make.

The biblical concept of love is best understood through concrete examples and practical illustrations. This is because the love of Christ, as has been noted, is a recognizable and observable quality. It is obvious in both its presence and its absence, as obvious as the qualities of salt and light. Because this is so, Christians have a readily identifiable trademark, as well as a practical gauge by which to indicate the genuineness of their faith and the measure of their growth:

> *Examine yourselves to see whether you are in the faith; test yourselves. Do you not realize that Christ Jesus is in you—unless, of course, you fail the test?* [111]

If a person is "in the faith," then Christ is dwelling in him or her, representatively, by His Spirit. On the other hand:

> *If anyone does not have the Spirit of Christ, he does not belong to Christ.*[112]

It has been previously mentioned that the indwelling pres-

---

[110]"For this very reason, make every effort to add to your faith..." (2 Peter 1:5-6; compare Heb. 11:6).
[111]2 Cor. 13:5.   [112]Rom. 8:9.

57

ence of the Spirit is shown by the fruit of the Spirit, which is a multifaceted, interrelational love. Those who are "keeping in step with the Spirit" are those who are walking in love. Biblical love is not a hit-and-miss proposition; it is a way of life to be decisively pursued:

And now I will show you the most excellent way.[113]

Follow the way of love....[114]

Be imitators of God, therefore, as dearly loved children and live a life of love....[115]

A Corrective Perspective

The example of the first-century Corinthian church provides a much needed perspective for present-day churches. The current egocentric emphasis on "my personal gift" and "my personal experience" has much in common with the Corinthian individualism that was negating both the unity of the local church and the basis of that unity, the love of Christ. This love had created the Christian community at Corinth, having been held out to the Corinthians in the gospel message and embraced by their common faith. (In this sense, love precedes faith in Christian experience, for if God had not "so loved the world" in Christ, we would have no Good News to believe!) This love was needed to "keep the unity of the Spirit through the bond of peace." But this love was being forgotten. It was being neglected and displaced to such an extent that Paul, in dealing with false teaching regarding the resurrection, had to remind the

---

[113]1 Cor. 12:31.   [114]1 Cor. 14:1.   [115]Eph. 5:1-2.

Corinthians of the gospel that had made them one in Christ.[116]

In their failure to hold to the priority of the love of God in Christ, the Corinthian church, which was certainly the most gifted church about which we read in the New Testament, had remained also the most immature, the most "flesh-dominated." Paul's first (extant) epistle to this church reveals a community rife with impatience and unkindness toward one another,[117] boastful pride,[118] jealousy,[119] vacillating loyalties,[120] moral insensitivity,[121] scandalous strife,[122] lack of brotherly consideration,[123] idolatrous flirtations,[124] self-centeredness,[125] self-promotion,[126] and doctrinal instability.[127] Obviously, it is possible for a congregation to be richly endowed with the *gifts* of the Spirit, while being at the same time destitute of the *fruit* of the Spirit.[128]

The Corinthian emphasis upon spiritual gifts and individualistic advancement demonstrated and perpetuated a condition of congregational immaturity. *The cure for this problem consisted then, as it does now, in a "body" perspective of the local church and its individual members, and the pursuit of love as the highest priority.* If a local church builds its life on any other basis than that of the love of Christ, there will be serious problems, as there were at Corinth. Many who claim to be Christians today are con-

---

[116]See 1 Cor. 15:1-8.
[117]See 1 Cor. 1:10-11.
[118]See 1 Cor. 1:29; 3:4.
[119]See 1 Cor. 3:3.
[120]See 1 Cor. 4:3-5.
[121]See 1 Cor. 5:1-2.
[122]See 1 Cor. 6:5-6.
[123]See 1 Cor. 8:9.
[124]See 1 Cor. 10:14.
[125]See 1 Cor. 11:17-22.
[126]See 1 Cor. 12:1-14:40.
[127]See 1 Cor. 15:1-58.
[128]See 1 Cor. 1:7; 13:1-3.

stantly pushing the miraculous spiritual gifts and individualistic spirituality. Yet an examination of their lives often reveals a hotbed of envy, pride, and even (as at Corinth) sexual immorality. If the core of local church life is anything other than the love of Christ, then the life of the local church is bound to be rotten at the core. Thus, a look at the early Corinthian church gives us a vivid portrait of what it means *not* to love one another as Christ has loved us.

The Ephesus Emphasis

The church at Ephesus provides another case in point concerning the crucial importance of faith, hope, and (above all) love in the health of the local church:

> *For this reason, ever since I heard about your faith in the Lord Jesus and your love for all the saints, I have not stopped giving thanks for you, remembering you in my prayers....I pray also that the eyes of your heart may be enlightened in order that you may know that hope to which he has called you....*[129]

> *As a prisoner for the Lord, then, I urge you to live a life worthy of the calling you have received. Be completely humble and gentle; be patient, bearing with one another in love. Make every effort to keep the unity of the Spirit through the bond of peace.*[130]

Paul was grateful to God for the love that flowed out of this church's sincere faith. He prayed that they might receive greater illumination concerning the exalted hope to which they had been called in Christ. But his admonition to these Christians—the burden of responsibility which he enjoined

---

[129]Eph. 1:15-16, 18.   [130]Eph. 4:1-3.

upon them—was that they maintain an attitude of gentleness and lowliness, and that they patiently bear with one another in love. Only through this love could self-centered ambition and pride be put away so that unity might prevail, as the Spirit of God had ordained. In the absence of this fruit of the Spirit (love), there can be only the divisive works of the flesh, a catalogue of corruption not unlike that which we have seen on display in the showroom of the Corinthian church:

> ...sexual immorality, impurity and debauchery; idolatry and witchcraft; hatred, discord, jealousy, fits of rage, selfish ambition, dissensions, factions and envy; drunkeness, orgies, and the like....Since we live by the Spirit, let us keep in step with the Spirit. Let us not become conceited, provoking and envying each other.[131]

Love And Christian Apologetics

All men will know that God has a people on the earth, and all will know that Jesus of Nazareth has true disciples in the world—if there is a demonstration of genuine loving relationships and true community among those who claim to follow Him. During the course of His so-called High Priestly prayer, Jesus emphasized the value of unity and love in commending the Christian faith to the world at large:

> "My prayer is not for them [the eleven] alone. I pray also for those who will believe in me through their message, that all of them may be one, Father, just as you are in me and I am in you. May they also be in us so that the world may believe that you have sent me."[132]

---

[131]Gal. 5:19-21, 25-26.   [132]John 17:20-21.

61

The maintenance and exhibition of this unity by loving one another with Christ's love is such a precious prize that it cannot be won without the willingness to pay a real price. The love of Christ is a subject which Christians can, and undoubtedly shall, talk about forever. However, the deepest knowledge is always reserved for those who practice the teaching,[133] and the practice of this teaching can be costly:

> *If any of you has a dispute with another, dare he take it before the ungodly for judgment instead of before the saints?...But instead, one brother goes to law against another—and this in front of unbelievers! The very fact that you have lawsuits among you means you have been completely defeated already. Why not rather be wronged? Why not rather be cheated?*[134]

Cultivating Love And Unity

Is Christian love and unity such a high priority for us that we would choose to forego financial gain, and even our rightful recompense, in order to attain it? In his Epistle to the Ephesians, Paul reminds us again that Christian unity, though graciously created by the Spirit in whom all Christians share, is something that must be maintained by diligent effort. Like a beautiful garden, it will not maintain itself:

> *Make every effort to keep the unity of the Spirit through the bond of peace.*[135]

It has been noted that balance is an important factor in cultivating a healthy congregation. The gardener must not become so involved in hoeing his tomatoes that he neglects watering his carrots. From its earliest days the Ephesian

---

[133]"If anyone chooses to do God's will, he will find out whether my teaching comes from God or whether I speak on my own" (John 7:17). [134]1 Cor. 6:1, 6-7.
[135]Eph. 4:3.

church apparently tended to swing from one extreme to another, being (in the words of Paul) "tossed back and forth by the waves, and blown here and there by every wind of teaching."[136] The Ephesians' initial enthusiasm was marked with a bonfire of public repentance from their former evil associations.[137] When Paul wrote his epistle to this church some eight years later, they apparently were growing together toward maturity, although Paul still looked forward to the day when their conformity to Christ would bring them to firm stability. The epistles to Timothy show that the second generation of Ephesian Christians was being plagued with Judaistic false teaching, as Paul had warned them only a few years earlier.[138] By the time the Spirit spoke to the Ephesian church through the Revelation of John, the problem of false teaching had been solved, but the risen Christ now had this against them: "You have forsaken your first love."[139]

The early history of the Ephesian church demonstrates that the maintenance of Christian unity requires earnest prayer, diligent effort, and careful balance.[140] Unity was not created by accident, nor will it be preserved by chance. God's people must deliberately give themselves to the pursuit of love while not neglecting truth. If we always aim at love as we hold firmly to truth, we will inevitably hit the mark of unity. When we consistently exhibit to the world at large practical love and unity in our relationships with one another, perhaps then the unreconciled will find it more difficult to ignore what we have been trying to say to them: that

---

[136]Eph. 4:14.   [137]See Acts 19:1-20.
[138]See Acts 20:29-31.   [139]Rev. 2:4.
[140]These matters are conveniently summarized by Steve Singleton, *Timothy and Titus Expanded Study Guide* (Clifton Park, NY: Life Communications, 1984), p. 15.

God has so loved the world that He has given His Son for the salvation of whoever will believe.

6

THE GREATNESS OF LOVE IN THE LOCAL CHURCH

And this is my prayer: that your love may abound more and more in knowledge and depth of insight, so that you may be able to discern what is best and may be pure and blameless until the day of Christ, filled with the fruit of righteousness that comes through Jesus Christ—to the glory and praise of God.[141]

In considering Paul's response to the numerous problems which plagued the Corinthian church, the question was raised: Why is love the greatest among all the distinctive characteristics of Christianity—even above faith and hope? One answer is that the power of love is indispensable in commending the gospel of Christ to a lost world. But the greatness of love does not reside merely in its "usefulness." Love that is offered merely as a means to an end (no matter how noble that end might be) is not worthy to be called "love."

At the same time, we must not be afraid to rejoice in the practical benefits that accompany a life of love. Love lived

---

[141]Phil. 1:9-11.

among the members of a Christian community—even a community of such dubious character as that of the Corinthian church—will have a definite, positive impact on the lives of its members, as well as on the world at large. In Paul's epistles to the churches of the first century, he never mentions any concern that they are to abound more and more in any particular program of evangelism, edification, or any such thing. He is always concerned with that which will promote and motivate the "reaching out" and the "building up": the love of Christ.

Love And Evangelism

Love is more than an evangelistic tool. In a very real sense, love *is* evangelism; nothing proclaims Christ as convincingly as a life of God-centered love. Consider once again Paul's famous celebration of love in 1 Corinthians 13. In this text, the name "Jesus" could easily be inserted in place of the word "love," without any sense of impropriety: "Jesus is patient, Jesus is kind. Jesus does not envy, He does not boast, He is not proud. Jesus is not rude, He is not self-seeking, He is not easily angered, He keeps no record of wrongs. Jesus does not delight in evil but rejoices with the truth."

In light of what has been said concerning the importance of testing ourselves as to whether we are truly in Christ and He in us, we could hardly devise a more revealing test than that of inserting our own names into Paul's "love chapter," as we have just done with the name of Jesus. Few exercises are likely to sober our minds and humble our hearts more than this one. I would personally urge the reader to set this book aside for the moment, open the Bible to 1 Corinthians 13, and take this test. If your life is characterized by the qualities of love that Paul describes here, then you are a walking, talking embodiment of the Good News about Jesus. (By the way, it *is* important for us to be talking as we are walking;[142] a transformed life requires some kind of explanation, and there is only one adequate explanation for this kind of life: the power of the gospel of Christ!)

Sold On "Tough Love"

Perhaps the reason why Christians do not practice greater love is that they are not completely sold on the greatness of love. "A man convinced against his will is of the same opinion still." Each one of us must ask himself whether he or she is really a believer in love. Many people claim to "believe in love," but they mean "love" in a superficial, sentimental sense: they cry at weddings, coo at babies, and get misty-eyed when the band plays "our song." But when it comes to "costly love"—the love that denies the will of self in order to do the will of God—the ranks of those who "believe in love" become considerably thinner:

> *Large crowds were traveling with Jesus, and turning to them he said: "If anyone comes to me and does not hate his father and mother, his wife and children, his brothers and sisters— yes, even his own life—he cannot be my disciple....In the same way, any of you who does not give up everything he has cannot be my disciple."* [143]

Currently, many who are rediscovering the true nature of Christian discipleship are saying and writing a lot about "tough love." It is difficult to imagine that any love could

---

[142]Matt. 28:19. The literal sense of this Greek construction is,"Therefore, while you are going, make disciples...."
[143]Luke 14:25-26, 33.

be tougher than that love to which Jesus calls us: a love that will allow no rival, no relationship, no responsibility to come between the disciple and his Lord. Yet, if the love of Christ is "tough," the refusal to love is much tougher. Lovelessness can only mean lifelessness:

> *Then he called the crowd to him along with his disciples and said:"If anyone would come after me, he must deny himself and take up his cross and follow me. For whoever wants to save his life will lose it, but whoever loses his life for me and for the gospel will save it."*[144]

Are we truly ready to commit our lives to genuine Christian discipleship? Are we serious about dying to self-will so that Christ can live in us? Will we, or will we not, "spend and be spent" in order that Christ Jesus may be lifted up and His gospel held forth? Have you and I been decisively sold on love as a personal life principle? In the following paragraphs, attention will be given to three reasons why love is the greatest biblical concept, and why each one of us should commit our lives to it.[145]

The Greatness Of Love

First, love is the greatest because it abides forever:

> *And now these three remain: faith, hope and love. But the greatest of these is love.*[146]

Love is eternal because God is eternal, and God is love:

---

[144]Mark 8:34-35.
[145]This writer is indebted to author Gene Getz for his formulation of these four points in *The Measure of a Church* (Ventura, CA: Regal Books, 1975), pp. 22-30.
[146]1 Cor. 13:13.

Whoever does not love does not know God, because God is love. This is how God showed his love among us: He sent his one and only Son into the world that we might live through him. This is love: not that we loved God, but that he loved us and sent his Son as an atoning sacrifice for our sins. Dear friends, since God so loved us, we also ought to love one another....God is love. Whoever lives in love lives in God, and God in him.[147]

The essential characteristic of God's moral nature is love. But God is not just the *word* "love"; He is the essence of all that truly *is* "love." His expression of love in the living and dying of Jesus is the full revelation of that love which is His very being. The definition and standard of love for the Christian is the action of God in Christ. Notice the precise formulation of the definition: "God is love." The Bible never says that "love is God"; that kind of statement is too open-ended, allowing man to make God in his own image, according to his own warped concept of what "love" is. Instead, the apostle carefully defines his terms: God is love, and love is the sacrificial, forgiving, reconciling act of God in Christ:

You see, at just the right time, when we were still powerless, Christ died for the ungodly. Very rarely will anyone die for a righteous man, though for a good man someone might possibly dare to die. But God demonstrates his own love for us in this: While we were still sinners, Christ died for us.[148]

All this is from God, who reconciled us to himself through Christ and gave us the ministry of reconciliation: that God was reconciling the world to himself in Christ, not counting men's sins against them....God made him who had no sin to be sin for us, so that in him we might become the righteousness of God.[149]

---

[147] 1 John 4:8-11, 16.   [148] Rom. 5:6-8.
[149] 2 Cor. 5:18-19, 21.

69

God gives of Himself to abundantly supply the needs of the undeserving and the disadvantaged. He is the God of all grace who became poor in Christ so that a morally bankrupt humanity might become spiritually rich. He became so mercifully involved in the problems and the pain occasioned by the sins of human beings that He took the whole mess upon Himself in order to free others of their burdens. This is the God who has many admirers, but far too few followers.

Why then should we love? We should love because we are striving to be imitators of the God who revealed Himself in Christ Jesus. We should love because God is love, and we who are in Christ have been made to share in His nature and in His Spirit.

Many people today are thinking in terms of sound investments for the future. God is offering us the ultimate investment opportunity: "Invest in eternity," He is urging us. "Liquidate all of your personal assets and become a shareholder in the divine nature by investing it all in love." This will mean (among other things): seeking and granting forgiveness freely; keeping no record of personal offenses against ourselves; doing without so that the needs of others can be supplied; keeping silent when we would speak, and speaking boldly when we would rather keep silent. The premiums are very high, but the return on this investment is phenomenal:

> And this is what he promised us—even eternal life.[150]

Love Versus The New Gnosticism

Second, love is the greatest because Jesus Himself called it the "first and greatest commandment":

---

[150]1 John 2:25.

Hearing that Jesus had silenced the Sadducees, the Pharisees got together. One of them, an expert in the law, tested him with this question: "Teacher, which is the greatest commandment in the Law?" Jesus replied: "'Love the Lord your God with all your heart and with all your soul and with all your mind.' This is the first and greatest commandment. And the second is like it: 'Love your neighbor as yourself.' All the Law and the Prophets hang on these two commandments." [151]

We are again confronted with the fact that this love can be, and is, commanded of us. It is more primarily a response of will than of emotion, but it encompasses the involvement of the whole person: "heart, soul, and mind." Even more pertinent to the present discussion is the inseparability of the first commandment from the second, as John later wrote:

We love because he first loved us. If anyone says, "I love God," yet hates his brother, he is a liar. For anyone who does not love his brother, whom he has seen, cannot love God, whom he has not seen. And he has given us this command: Whoever loves God must also love his brother. [152]

John was addressing the Gnostic tendency to exalt knowledge over love, and to extol the heavenly and the divine while despising the earthly and the human. Jesus, however, dealt with Pharisees who, in their self-righteous egotism and pomposity, attempted to maintain that same dichotomy: loving God while loathing their fellow human beings. [153] Today, we see a type of neo-gnosticism, a contemporary

---

[151] Matt. 22:34-40. Jesus cites Deut. 6:5 and Lev. 19:18, respectively.

[152] 1 John 4:19-21.

[153] For examples of this spirit, Luke's gospel account is particularly useful (see Luke 5:27-31; 7:36-50; 15:1-32; 18:9-14).

Pharisaism, in the midst of the modern local congregation as some who claim to wear the name of Christ try to worship God acceptably while hating those who are made in His image. Racial and ethnic prejudices and bias regarding customs and cultures stand as painful proof of this problem of not fully accepting brethren in Christ. Personal disputes between members of the same congregation often remain unresolved, as one generation hands them down to the next. Doctrinal differences among those who truly belong to Christ continue to result in multiple splinters and fractures of the body of Christ, ranging in degree from cliques and sectarian subcommunities to full-blown denominational divisions. And do we wonder why the present generation is not listening to us?

James also exposed this hypocritical approach to God among the members of the Jewish Christian community which he addressed:

> *With the tongue we praise our Lord and Father, and with it we curse men, who have been made in God's likeness. Out of the same mouth come praise and cursing. My brothers, this should not be.*[154]

The second commandment (love for neighbor) is "like" the first (love for God), said Jesus. James reminds us that this is because man is "like" God: made in His image and likeness. What we do (or refuse to do) for our brothers, we do also for our Lord. Even if a person is not our brother in Christ, our obligation to love him remains, for he is still our "neighbor"; we are to love him and do good to him.[155] It cannot be simply "verbal love." It must be love "with ac-

---

[154]James 3:9-10.
[155]See Luke 10:25-37; Rom. 12:14, 17-21; 1 Cor. 10:31-33; Gal. 6:10; 1 Thess. 5:15; Titus 3:1-2.

tions and in truth";[156] it must be (as someone once put it) "love with skin on it."

Love, Lust, And Legalism

How free and generous we can be with our words! "Certainly, I love him. He's my neighbor, isn't he?" "Of course, I care for her. She's my sister!" But the question must be asked: "Why, then, do our actions so consistently fail to confirm our words?" If there is really love in one's heart—a husband for his wife; a parent for a child; a Christian for his neighbor—it will somehow be manifested outwardly. Love, in any of its qualities and types, refuses to remain anonymous. Consider God's love for mankind, and for each of us personally. The Father did not simply say to us, "Even though you have been an ungrateful, self-centered, sinful creature who has made a mess of this wonderful gift of life which I have entrusted to you (to say nothing of this beautiful planet which I created for you), I just want you to know: I love you. Of course, since you have sown to your own flesh, you must reap death and corruption, and be separated from Me eternally. But, I repeat: I do really love you. I have such great love for you, deep down in My heart." God did not merely theorize about loving man. The love of God is never theoretical; it is always active and practical.

How do we know that God loved? Almost any third grade Sunday school student can tell you the answer:

---

[156] 1 John 3:18.

73

"For God so loved the world that he gave his one and only Son, that whoever believes in him shall not perish but have eternal life." [157]

We know that God loved because "He gave"—He gave! Self-centered man wants to seize, to grab, to take. His motivation is the very opposite of love. It is lust: selfish desire. This self-centered egotism, fueled by the proud pursuit of legalistic righteousness (such as was being promoted by Judaistic false teachers among the Galatian churches), is that which stands opposed to the love of Christ and which threatens to dismember the body of Christ, tearing one joint from another as each member goes its own self-willed way:

> *You, my brothers, were called to be free. But do not use your freedom to indulge the sinful nature* [flesh]; *rather, serve one another in love. The entire law is summed up in a single command: "Love your neighbor as yourself." If you keep on biting and devouring each other, watch out or you will be destroyed by each other.* [158]

The concept of servanthood is vitally related to that of love. People can be compelled to obey by a show of force, but they cannot be truly motivated to serve, except by love. Since God in Christ has become the Servant of all, His authority and example binds the followers of Christ to love (and serve) one another:

> *Let no debt remain outstanding, except the continuing debt to love one another, for he who loves his fellow man has fulfilled the law. The commandments, "Do not commit adultery," "Do not murder," "Do not steal," "Do not covet," and whatever other commandment there may be, are summed up in this one*

---

[157]John 3:16.   [158]Gal. 5:13-15.

74

rule: "Love your neighbor as yourself." Love does no harm to its neighbor. Therefore love is the fulfillment of the law.[159]

Most of us owe the government a percentage of our personal income, which we call "tax." When you pay your taxes, you become free of that debt—at least until the following year! Similarly, if you were to buy a car and arrange for a three-year payment plan, you could theoretically be free of that debt at the end of the three years. You could produce a receipt, upon request, which would say something to this effect: "Paid in full." But our obligation to love those who are made in God's image, who are of our own "kind," for whom also Christ died, is a debt from which we can never be free. And here is the greatness of love: Though it never ceases to be required of us, it also never fails to meet the requirement of God's law. Paul and Jesus agree that divine love is the standard for determining the spirit, the intent, of God's law. Actions and attitudes which flow out from a heart filled with divine love can only do good, and not harm, to any human being. The well-being of man is the intent of God's law, and love fulfills that intent.[160]

---

[159]Rom. 13:8-10.

[160]The mistake of the Pharisees in their approach to righteousness was their perception of the Law as their ultimate master, as an end in itself rather than as the means by which loving service to God should be rendered. The result was that they had practically divorced the Person of God from their understanding of the Law (see Matt. 5:17-20; 12:1-2; and Luke 11:42, 52).

What's It All About?

Third, love is the greatest because it is the most frequently repeated command and exhortation in the New Testament, occurring no less than fifty-five times.[161] Yet, in my almost thirty years as a Christian, I have heard many more sermons about repentance and baptism (which certainly are important biblical subjects) than I have heard about love. One would almost conclude that the Bible is a book about baptism instead of a book about God's redeeming love. I do not want to hear less about other biblical matters, but more about love! We should adjust the content of our preaching and teaching to coincide proportionately with the content of Scripture. All other biblical commandments fall into proper perspective when we understand and apply the commandment of love.

"If you love me, you will obey what I command." [162]

This is love for God: to obey his commands. And his commands are not burdensome....[163]

Many who claim to be Christ's do not keep His commands. They would disagree with the apostle's claim that "his commands are not burdensome." This is usually because they have distorted the commandments of Jesus into a straitlaced legal system, having nothing to do with love for the Lord. Such people need to understand that love for God cannot be separated from obedience to Him, for "this is love for God: to obey his commands." If I love God, my question will not

---

[161]See Matt. 5:44; 22:39; John 13:34; 1 Cor. 14:1; 16:14; Gal. 5:13; Eph. 4:2, 15; 5:2, 25; Phil. 2:2ff; Col. 3:12-14; 2 Tim. 2:22; Heb. 10:24; 1 Peter 2:17; 4:8; 1 John 3:18.
[162]John 14:15.   [163]1 John 5:3.

76

take the form, "What do I have to do?" One who truly loves the Father and the Son will desire, above all else, to obey His commands. This is the response of the loving disciple: "Lord, whatever pleases You is what I want to do with all of my heart, soul, and mind." Why? Because the genuine disciple loves the One who first loved him:

> The life I live in the body, I live by faith in the Son of God, who loved me and gave himself for me.[164]

> For Christ's love compels us, because we are convinced that one died for all, and therefore all died. And he died for all, that those who live should no longer live for themselves but for him who died for them and was raised again.[165]

> My purpose is that they may be encouraged in heart and united in love, so they may have the full riches of complete understanding, in order that they may know the mystery of God, namely, Christ, in whom are hidden all the treasures of wisdom and knowledge.[166]

> Instead, speaking the truth in love, we will in all things grow up into him who is the head, that is, Christ. From him the whole body, joined and held together by every supporting ligament, grows and builds itself up in love, as each part does its work.[167]

These passages summarize the theme of this entire volume. If the members of the local church really learn how to love one another, they will grow up into the likeness of Christ, but it will not happen unless the members become personally committed to the love of Christ as the guiding principle of their

---

[164]Gal. 2:20.   [165]2 Cor. 5:14-15.
[166]Col. 2:2-3.   [167]Eph. 4:15-16.

77

lives. Let us be done with all of the shortcuts and gimmicks which propose to offer us growth without inconvenience, sacrifice, and pain. Let us refuse to succumb to the worldly spirit of pragmatism, which quickly endorses whatever method seems to "get the job done." In Christ, God has loved the unlovely unconditionally, and He calls us to love one another even as we have been loved.

7

THE BEHAVIOR OF LOVE IN THE LOCAL CHURCH

It was just before the Passover Feast. Jesus knew that the time had come for him to leave this world and go to the Father. Having loved his own who were in the world, he now showed them the full extent of his love. The evening meal was being served, and the devil had already prompted Judas Iscariot, son of Simon, to betray Jesus. Jesus knew that the Father had put all things under his power, and that he had come from God and was returning to God; so he got up from the meal, took off his outer clothing, and wrapped a towel around his waist. After that, he poured water into a basin and began to wash his disciples' feet, drying them with the towel that was wrapped around him.[168]

"Who Wrote The Book Of Love?"

The Gospel of John bears all the marks of being an authentic eyewitness testimony, which is exactly what the book claims for itself.[169] In the incarnation of Christ, God and His great love

---

[168] John 13:1-5.
[169] See John 1:1-4; 19:35; 20:30-31; 21:24.

for all mankind have been fully revealed. John's written record of the words and deeds of Jesus, though by no means exhaustive, is nevertheless a sufficient medium through which the Spirit of God can bring the honest enquirer to saving faith. When we compare John's gospel account with the synoptics, we are confronted with many questions about chronology, historical detail, and theology. However, differences between John and the Synoptics pose no insurmountable problems to either the historian or the theologian, and should not prevent us from seeing these portraits of Jesus as complementary, rather than contradictory.

Love Is Patient

Jesus' issuing of the "new commandment" to His disciples is unique to John's gospel account, but its impact can be fully appreciated only when the historical situation in which it was given is carefully considered: "As I have loved you, so you must love one another." By comparing the parallel accounts in Matthew, Mark, and Luke with the occasion described by John ("it was just before the Passover feast"), a coherent picture begins to emerge. Jesus was preparing to eat the Passover meal with His disciples, as He had "eagerly desired" to do in preparation for His passion.[170]

As the disciples entered the upper room, they could not have failed to notice the water pitcher, bowl, and towel which had been furnished for the purpose of washing the feet of the guests as they came in from the dusty roads. (In first-century

---

[170]See Luke 22:15. Jesus apparently ate the meal prior to the actual appointed day, knowing that His death would preclude His participation on the day.

80

Palestine, this customary courtesy was often performed by the household slave.)

They had all met there at the bidding of their Teacher: Peter, James, John, and the other disciples. It is not difficult to imagine them, nudging and elbowing their way toward the place of honor next to their divine Host, as the whole situation degenerated into a pathetic debate concerning "which of them was considered to be the greatest."[171]

Probably nobody noticed the strange quietness of Judas Iscariot, son of Simon.

These men had been with Jesus for the better part of three years. They had witnessed His relentless selflessness. They had heard His great teaching: the parables of the kingdom of God; the Sermon on the Mount; the remarkable replies to His enemies who sought to silence and condemn Him on legal grounds. He had spoken to them often concerning their unique relationship to one another as His disciples. Nevertheless, here they are, at the end of the three appointed years of flawless teaching and role modeling: a spectacle of petty self-promotion.

Love On Its Knees

The room is prepared, but there is no house servant to perform the customary courtesy of foot washing. The meal is being served, but the feet of the guests remain dirty. Not one of the disciples makes a move to honor the Master by discharging the role of the servant in this matter. During supper, when it has

[171]See Luke 22:24-25.

become obvious that those who call Him "Lord" and "Teacher" have failed to appreciate the implication of their confession, Jesus—the Word of God incarnate—arises from the table, removes His outer garment, girds Himself with a towel, pours water into the wash bowl, gets down on His knees before His students and begins to wash their dirty feet, "drying them with the towel that was wrapped around Him." Having dealt with Peter's "humble" protest, and returning to His place at the table, Jesus makes the application for His disciples:

> *"Do you understand what I have done for you?" he asked them. "You call me 'Teacher' and 'Lord,' and rightly so, for that is what I am. Now that I, your Lord and Teacher, have washed your feet, you also should wash one another's feet. I have set you an example that you should do as I have done for you. I tell you the truth, no servant is greater than his master, nor is a messenger greater than the one who sent him. Now that you know these things, you will be blessed if you do them."* [172]

As usual, Jesus removes "love" from the realm of the theoretical and places it into the arena of the "real world." How do we know that Jesus was loving His disciples? Is it because He spoke so eloquently about His love for them? When we would offer platitudes, Jesus offers a pattern—a practical demonstration of love by the Teacher that any disciple can see and imitate. This was exactly what the messengers of Jesus needed then, and it is precisely what we need to see now, so that we might be convinced, once for all, that whatever is not too menial for the Master is not too menial for the servant.

Love And Leadership

With this "shocking" display of selfless service and shameless

---
[172]John 13:12-17.

humility, our Lord jolts us into rethinking our worldly concepts of "leadership" and "greatness":

> *"The kings of the Gentiles lord it over them; and those who exercise authority over them call themselves Benefactors. But you are not to be like that. Instead, the greatest among you should be like the youngest, and the one who rules like the one who serves. For who is greater, the one who is at the table or the one who serves? Is it not the one who is at the table? But I am among you as one who serves."* [173]

The Host of the feast has become the household slave: everything has been turned upside down! Or perhaps it is the kingdoms of this world which are upside down, and Jesus and His kingdom only appear to be so, from our egotistical perspective.

How many times have you and I thought to ourselves, "Me? Get down on my knees and serve that person?" To bring the point a bit closer to earth (and without meaning to be crude): some Christians seem to think themselves to be "above" cleaning the restrooms in the church building. An exaggerated sense of self-importance is a heavy load to carry through life. John's portrait of God on His knees, washing feet, should suffice to free us of this crippling burden once and for all. It is no wonder that Peter, limited as his perception was at the time, protested the apparent unseemliness of the situation. Jesus' reply to Peter's objection is both sobering and motivating:

> *"Unless I wash you, you have no part with me."* [174]

---

[173] Luke 22:25-27.　　　　　[174] John 13:8.

83

Love In The Local Congregation

The "new commandment" was not spoken in a vacuum. It had a context; it arose out of a particular situation and a specific need. Soon the disciples would become "the messengers," and the quality of their behavior toward one another would be decisive in determining their impact on the world at large:

> *"A new command I give you: Love one another. As I have loved you, so you must love one another. All men will know that you are my disciples if you love one another."* [175]

Those who claim to be members of Christ's body, those who "have a part" with Jesus (having been "washed" through His blood) must honestly ask themselves: Am I loving, even as Jesus has loved me? Do I demonstrate the love for my brothers and sisters in Christ which Jesus has shown to me, in that He gave Himself up completely to serve me in my most desperate need? How can I experience and express the love of Christ to my fellow disciples in the practical context of the local congregation?

It is my belief that our answers to these questions should be given only after a serious consideration of the various "one another" passages located throughout the New Testament. In the New Testament writings, the Spirit of Jesus speaks through His apostles and prophets to apply the love of Christ to specific problems and needs within various first century congregations. The detailed study and practical application of these "one another" texts extend beyond the scope of this section, but I offer the following list in order to acquaint the reader

---

[175] John 13:34-35.

84

with the breadth of this teaching, and to introduce some of the relevant passages:

1. Cooperating with and caring for one another (1 Cor. 12:19-25).

2. Service motivated by love for one another (Gal. 5:13).

3. Bearing with one another "in love" (Eph. 4:2).

4. Bearing one another's burdens (Gal. 6:2; 1 Cor. 12:26).

5. Encouraging one another (1 Thess. 5:11; Heb. 3:12-13; 10:24-25).

6. Submitting to one another (Eph. 5:21).

7. Forgiving one another (Eph. 4:32; Col. 3:13; see also Matt. 18:21ff.).

8. Being honest with one another (Eph. 4:14, 25; Col. 3:9-10; James 5:9).

9. Showing hospitality to one another (1 Peter 4:9).

10. Teaching and admonishing one another (Eph. 5:19; Col. 3:16).

11. Confessing our sins to one another and praying for one another (James 5:16).

This list is only a representative sampling of the "one another" flavor that permeates the New Testament. However, it is sufficient to show that there are many commandments included within the "new commandment."

Cohesive Love

"No messenger is greater than the one who sent him," said Jesus. His concern was that this bickering batch of competitive egos would see in Him the motivation and example that could transform them into a loving and united community, thus enabling them to be effective in bringing His saving message to a dying world.

Consider the group of disciples whose feet Jesus washed that night. There were tax-paying fishermen, a publican who gathered revenues for Rome, and a Zealot who had hated Rome as the very embodiment of all that opposed God. There were the clannish sons of Zebedee, who sent their mother to Jesus with an outrageous request for personal glory that infuriated the other disciples. And there was Judas Iscariot, the only Judean of the lot, who was even at that time totally committed to the will of Satan, having determined to deliver Jesus into the hands of those who plotted His death. A more unlikely assortment of backgrounds, occupations, and perspectives would be difficult to assemble, and all but impossible to unify around a common cause. Only a personality as powerful as that of the Son of God could provide an adequate center for such a community. He held them together by the power of His love. He washed each one of them, and each one of them, with the obvious exception of the betrayer, was personally committed to the same cause: Jesus Christ. Differences, deep and numerous, remained among them; but they had one thing in common: They loved and trusted Jesus of Nazareth.

Can we not see the application of these things to the problems that threaten the unity of the Spirit in today's local churches?

Almost every case of congregational infighting and division that I have ever seen has been caused by a stubborn, self-willed refusal by some members to receive one another and to accept one another in non-essential matters. There have been only a very few exceptions in my experience, where Christians had to stand for certain biblical absolutes,[176] and there had to be a parting of the ways:

> *They went out from us, but they did not really belong to us. For if they had belonged to us, they would have remained with us; but their going showed that none of them belonged to us.*[177]

There are those cases (though I believe them to be rare) in which churches must divide because one group desires to remain faithful to the Lord, while another group has chosen to go its own way. But far more often, divisions occur as a result of intolerant, unloving, non-accepting attitudes toward those whose socio-economic background, skin color, hair length, dress style, and personal tastes differ from our own.

Accepting Love

In dealing with the problems of integrating the Jewish and Gentile elements that made up the Christian community at Rome, Paul gave this admonition by the Spirit of God:

---

[176] The kind of behavior that severs us from fellowship with God and with one another is clearly outlined in passages such as 1 Cor. 5:9-11; 6:9-10; Gal. 5:19-21; Eph. 5:3-7; 1 John 3:7-10. Doctrinal errors that produce the same result are as easily seen in such texts as Gal. 1:6-10; 5:2-4; Eph. 4:4-6; 1 Cor. 12:13; 15:1-19; 2 John 9-11.
[177] 1 John 2:19.

Accept him whose faith is weak, without passing judgment on disputable matters.[178]

We who are strong ought to bear with the failings of the weak and not to please ourselves. Each of us should please his neighbor for his good, to build him up. For even Christ did not please himself....May the God who gives endurance and encouragement give you a spirit of unity among yourselves as you follow Christ Jesus, so that with one heart and mouth you may glorify the God and Father of our Lord Jesus Christ. Accept one another, then, just as Christ accepted you, in order to bring. praise to God.[179]

This command to "accept one another" can be violated in two distinct ways: by *legalism* and by *liberalism*. Legalism is the making of laws in matters where God has not bound us. Liberalism is the ignoring of boundaries that God has set. The former problem restricts us from accepting into our fellowship those whom God accepts "in Christ." The latter deceives us into embracing as brothers and sisters those whom God has not received as His sons and daughters "in Christ."

The decisive issue, then, is not whether another individual shares my recreational interests, cultural background, economic status, or even my theological and moral peculiarities. The ultimate question is: Has Christ washed this person? Has God accepted him or her "in Christ"? Is he Christ's? If he is Christ's, then he must be mine, as well.

He came to Simon Peter, who said to him, "Lord, are you going to wash my feet?" Jesus replied, "You do not realize now what I am doing, but later you will understand." [180]

---

[178]Rom. 14:1.
[179]Rom. 15:1-3, 5-7.
[180]John 13:6-7.

Toward the end of his life, Peter still remembered the Man who was God, kneeling before him with the towel wrapped around His waist. He wrote:

Clothe yourselves with humility toward one another, because, "God opposes the proud but gives grace to the humble." [181]

May God grant us the grace to understand, even as Peter eventually came to understand, the wonderful thing that Jesus Christ has done for each of us by His towel and by His cross in bringing us together to be loving members, one of another.

---

[181] 1 Peter 5:5.

SCRIPTURE INDEX

(**Bold** type shows direct quotations)

(The Love Of Christ In TheLocal Congregation)

93

We Are One

If just once I could know
How it feels to be a part
Of a body that is one in heart and soul,
Then the Lord would smile on us,
Count us faithful to His trust
Of the precious blood of Jesus Christ, His Son.

Fellow people of God,
Won't you flow together now?
Be the church that Jesus Christ died to save!
Children of the Most High God,
He has called us each to die
And become the lovely body of the Lord.

If the people who love God
And claim Jesus as their Lord
Would deny their silly doctrines that divide,
If we all would recognize
That the business of our Lord
Is much more than playing church on Sunday morn!

We are one! We are one!
Don't you see the walls we've made
Are in our minds?
We are one in the Son;
Let the children that are free
Remind both you and me that we are one!

©1988 by Keith and Sanna Luker

Part Two

The Life of Christ

We Share:

Members One of

Another

*"There can be
no true family of man
unless it is
the family of God."*

Introductory Reflections: Part Two

I once read a book entitled *Great Church Fights.* At the time I remember thinking that a member of any religious group could have written such a book. *"We"* could have written it as well as *"they"!*

It is a sad and disgraceful thing when the people of God— whom God has called together to love, support, and serve one another in oneness—do otherwise. *God* is not the author of confusion.

It is hoped that this book may, in some way, help us who follow Christ to better appreciate the meaning of being *Members One of Another.* If we do, it will enhance the reality of our lives together in the Lord and bring unspeakable joy to that which God has called us to share.

Larry Deason

8

WHAT WE SHARE

The "one another" concept is explicitly cited over forty times in the New Testament. In the majority of its occurrences, it is derived from the Greek word *allelon,* and describes a reciprocal relationship between two (or more) persons: "one of another," "one from another," or "one toward another." There are about six cases where the "one another" idea is translated from the plural of the personal pronoun *heautou* : "to yourselves," "among yourselves." Both terms refer to various aspects of the relationship that exists among disciples of Jesus Christ, especially on the practical level of the local congregation.

In the preceding section, *The Love of Christ in the Local Congregation,* I examined in some detail the biblical teaching concerning the local church, and the nature and necessity of the love of Christ among its members. What was presented in theory in that section is applied practically in this one. It is essential that, having grasped the preeminence of love as the measure of maturity for any local church, we begin to experience and express the love of Christ in our relationships "one to another."

Endless Love

In virtually every situation where interpersonal problems existed in the local congregations of the New Testament, the apostolic response is an admonishment to call love to the forefront. Biblical love—the love of Christ—is consistently presented as the key to healthy relationships among members of the body of Christ.

> *Love never fails. But where there are prophecies, they will cease; where there are tongues, they will be stilled; where there is knowledge, it will pass away....And now, these three remain: faith, hope and love. But the greatest of these is love.*[1]

A study of the chronology of the New Testament letters reveals that those which are latest in date of composition increasingly emphasize, not miraculous spiritual gifts and manifestations, but spiritual fruit which is rooted in faith, hope, and love.[2] In another place I have noted that "love is the greatest" because it is of God and, like Him, will abide forever.[3] It will never become superfluous, obsolete, or irrelevant. Like the Son of God who is its full embodiment, love "is the same yesterday and today and forever."[4]

---

[1] 1 Cor. 13:8, 13.

[2] These would include Paul's Captivity Epistles (c. A.D. 61-63), Pastoral Epistles (c. A.D. 63-67), the Epistle to the Hebrews (c. A.D. 64), the First Epistle of Peter (c. A.D. 62-64), the Second Epistle of Peter (c. A.D. 68), the Johannine Epistles (c. 90-95), and the Epistle of Jude (c. A.D. 65-85). These dates were suggested by Donald Guthrie (*New Testament Introduction* [Downers Grove, IL: Inter-Varsity Press, 1970], pp. 666, 717, 796, 850, 883, 912).

[3] Larry Deason, *The Love of Christ in the Local Congregation* (Clifton Park, NY: Life Communications, 1987), p. 60.

[4] This divine attribute is ascribed to Jesus Christ in Heb. 13:8.

Where Love Is Found

The congregation planted by Paul at Corinth lacked no spiritual gift. They had all manner of divine endowments, both natural (such as believing God and helping others) and supernatural (such as performing miracles, receiving divine revelations, and speaking in unlearned foreign languages).[5] But although they were rich in the Spirit's gifts, they were desperately poor in His fruit. Therefore the diversity, which (by God's design) was to have resulted in the members serving one another and growing up together into the image of Jesus Christ, had instead produced a disfigured and divided body.

The members of the body were not surrendering themselves to the authority of their benevolent Head. Each member was going its own self-willed way, and the only cure for this "spastic" condition was an immediate and massive application of the love of Christ, one member to another, throughout the whole body. This precious antidote has been made abundantly available to "whosoever will" by the Great Physician at Calvary's cross. He Himself has absorbed the entire cost of the treatment program, and has written our prescription in His own blood. Members of the reconciled body have unlimited access to His healing, cleansing love:

> *And hope does not disappoint us, because God has poured out his love into our hearts by the Holy Spirit, whom he has given*

---

[5]See 1 Cor. 12:7-11, 27-30. These gifts bestowed by the Spirit to members of the body of Christ are presented as functions in the church which have been appointed by God.

us....God demonstrates his own love for us in this: While we were still sinners, Christ died for us. Since we have now been justified by his blood, how much more shall we be saved from God's wrath through him! For if, when we were God's enemies, we were reconciled to him through the death of his Son, how much more, having been reconciled, shall we be saved through his life![6]

The Care Of God's Extended Family

The Bible, without apology, tells us that "God is love."[7] He didn't "become" love when the Son of God became flesh and dwelt among us; rather, the incarnation revealed the moral nature and glory of the God who never changes:

God said to Moses, "I am who I am. This is what you are to say to the Israelites: 'I AM has sent me to you'"[8]

"I the LORD do not change. So you, O descendants of Jacob, are not destroyed."[9]

"I tell you the truth," Jesus answered, "before Abraham was born, I am!"[10]

"Love" requires an object—someone(s) to love. The Godhead is a self-contained community of love: an eternal relationship of mutual love among the Persons of the Godhead. God did not need to *create* someone to love in order to become a loving God:

*In the beginning was the Word, and the Word was with God, and the Word was God. He was with God in the beginning....
The Word became flesh and lived for awhile among us.*[11]

------

[6]Rom. 5:5, 8-10. [7]1 John 4:8,16. [8]Exod. 3:14.
[9]Mal. 3:6. [10]John 8:58. [11]John 1:1-2, 14.

"And now, Father, glorify me in your presence with the glory I had with you before the world began....I have given them the glory that you gave me, that they may be one as we are one: I in them and you in me....Father, I want those you have given me to be with me where I am, and to see my glory, the glory you have given me because you loved me before the creation of the world." [12]

Within this infinite affiliation of love, there is an eternal purpose and plan. It is impossible to comprehend the mode of a transcendent interaction, but biblical revelation is clear on the point that promises were made within the Godhead "before the beginning of time."[13] God's omniscience encompassed the moral failure of His human creatures, and His omnipotence guided salvation throughout history to a climax in the incarnation of Christ and the establishment of His church. Thus were God's promises to the Jewish patriarchs ultimately fulfilled: Jesus Christ, the risen Son of Abraham and of David, has become the center of God's "extended family," composed of those from all nations who are reconciled to God in Him:

The promises were spoken to Abraham and to his seed. The Scripture does not say "and to seeds," meaning many people, but "and to your seed," meaning one person, who is Christ....You are all sons of God through faith in Christ Jesus, for all of you who were baptized into Christ have clothed yourselves with Christ. There is neither Jew nor Greek, slave nor free, male nor female, for you are all one in Christ Jesus. If you belong to Christ, then you are Abraham's seed, and

---

[12]John 17:5, 22-24.
[13]Titus 1:1-3 and compare 2 Tim. 1:8-11; 1 Peter 1:18-21; Eph. 1:3-14; 3:1-12; Rom. 8:28-30; 16:25-27; 1 Cor. 2:6-8; Col. 1:24-27. See Larry Deason, *The Eternal Purpose and Plan of God* (Clifton Park, NY: Life Communications, 1990).

heirs according to the promise.[14]

The Myth Of Man, The Misfit

It is essential for us to understand that God *wants* each one of His children. We were chosen in Christ before time began, and we were redeemed by Him in the fullness of time. Being complete in Himself, God was under no compulsion to create man, much less to adopt him in Jesus at such a great cost. Contrary to the darkened understanding of the modern unbelieving mind, man is not "born by accident and dead by design," nor is the church of Christ a chance occurrence within a meaningless historical process. There is not a single one of His children whom God did not foreknow. The family of God has its "roots" in the pre-creation relationship of the Father, Son, and Spirit, and will continue throughout eternity.

The adopted members of this family share in a unique and distinctive legacy that comes due to their position as those who are "in Christ." It is this common heritage that defines the meaning of Paul's inspired phrase, "members one of another," and which forms the basis for all of the privileges and responsibilities implied by that phrase. What do we who are "in Christ" share together, as members one of another? The following ten answers to this question are not intended to exhaust our thinking concerning our common reality "in Christ," but are offered to stimulate its further

[14]Gal. 3:16, 26-29. See also Gal. 3:6-9; 4:1-7, 21-31; Matt. 1:1ff; 8:11; Acts 2:29ff; 13:22-23, 32-39; 15:14-18; Rom. 1:6; 4:13-25; 1 Cor.12:13; 2 Cor. 5:14-21; Eph. 2:11-22; Col. 1:18-23; 3:11-14; 2 Tim. 2:8.

consideration. A clear appreciation of the meaning and depth of *brotherhood in Christ* is imperative for a consistent, practical application of "one another" principles.

The Same Gospel

First, we who are in Christ are "members one of another" because we have obeyed the *same gospel:*

> *Now, brothers, I want to remind you of the gospel I preached to you, which you received and on which you have taken your stand. By this gospel you are saved, if you hold firmly to the word I preached to you. Otherwise, you have believed in vain. For what I received I passed on to you as of first importance: that Christ died for our sins according to the Scriptures, that he was buried, that he was raised on the third day according to the Scriptures, and that he appeared....* [15]

> *I am astonished that you are so quickly deserting the one who called you by the grace of Christ and are turning to a different gospel—which is really no gospel at all.* [16]

In considering this matter of membership in the family of God, there are certain definite priorities, and a shared personal commitment to the same Good News is "of first importance." The close textual relationship between Paul's addressing of the Corinthians as "brothers" and his reviewing the Good News as he had proclaimed it to them is not merely coincidental. The Corinthians were "brothers" on the basis of the gospel concerning Christ's death for sins, His burial, and His bodily resurrection. Their relationship to

---

[15]1 Cor. 15:1-5.   [16]Gal. 1:6-7.

108

God and to one another "in Christ" was contingent[17] upon their personal continuance in what later came to be called "the faith."[18]

The message concerning Christ's manifested victory over sin and death was understood as the realization of the gospel of the kingdom of God, which had permeated the teaching of John the Baptizer[19] and Jesus of Nazareth. This Good News concerning the triumph of God's enthroned Messiah demands an "obedience of faith" which involves the whole person. The biblical response of "faith" requires an intellectual conviction that the crucified Jesus is now the risen Lord and divine Savior ("belief"), and a decision to change the moral direction of one's entire life on the basis of recognition of Jesus as Lord ("repentance"). But "obeying the gospel"[20] goes beyond mere mental assent and moral decision. It involves an embodiment of the Good News of Jesus which begins with our imitation of His death, burial, and resurrection in baptism, and continues in a daily public acknowledgement of Jesus as Lord of our lives.[21]

---

[17]This same contingency is noted in Col. 1:22-23.

[18]The expression "the faith" was already in use by Paul as a synonym for "the gospel" as early as A.D. 52 (Gal. 1:23). It is listed among seven essentials of Christian unity outlined by Paul in Eph. 4:4-6. By the time of the writing of the Pastorals, "the faith" has become Paul's usual term denoting "the gospel" (1 Tim. 1:2; 3:9; 4:1, 6; 5:8; 6:10, 21; 2 Tim. 3:8; 4:7; Titus 1:13). See also Jude 3.

[19]The phrase "John the Baptizer" is preferred over the more traditional "John the Baptist."

[20]See Rom. 6:17; 2 Thess. 1:8; 1 Peter 1:2, 22; 4:17.

[21]See Rom. 6:1-3; 10:9-10. Luke's description of conversion and Christian discipleship in the Book of Acts conforms to the infor-

All members of the family of God are disciples of Jesus. If we have not responded obediently to the same gospel—the "truth of the gospel," which is Christ crucified for sins and exalted as Lord—then we are not members one of another, we do not belong to the same body, and we are not brothers and sisters in Christ. If, on the other hand, we are continuing in our obedience to the Good News of God's grace toward us in Christ, it is obvious that we are members one of another, for this gospel is the means by which God calls us to become His children.[22]

If Christ Himself is our "bronze serpent" to whom we must look for the healing of our broken relationships with God and man, then the gospel of Him "lifted up" (first, on the cross, and then to the Father's right hand) is surely the standard on which He is held out for our contemplation as the object of saving faith.[23]

The Same Family

Second, "members one of another" means that those who are in Christ are members of the *same family:*

> ....*if I am delayed, you will know how people ought to conduct themselves in God's household, which is the church of the*

---

mation gleaned from Paul's epistles, when the terms and theological perspectives of both writers are properly understood. Luke's distinctive terminology in discussing the Holy Spirit has caused some to mistakenly conclude that he is inconsistent with Paul and with himself in his descriptions of the beginning of Christian life. The reader is urged to study carefully the Acts accounts of conversions to Christ, paying special attention to how Luke uses such phrases as "received the Holy Spirit," "the Holy Spirit fell on them," "the gift of the Holy Spirit," etc.

[22]See 2 Thess. 2:13-14.   [23]See John 3:14-15; Num. 21:4-9.

living God, the pillar and foundation of the truth.[24]

In his explanation of purpose in writing the letter we call "First Timothy," Paul clearly states that his concept of the church of God is that of a *family*, a perspective which was also dominant in the mind of Christ.[25] Many of our modern problems and controversies concerning such issues as the role of women in the church, the qualifications for church leaders, and the meaning of "headship" can be traced to an inadequate appreciation of the church as "God's household." A perception of every Christian household as a "church in miniature" could go a long way in exposing and correcting many inconsistencies and misconceptions about how men, women, and children "ought to conduct themselves in church": that is, how each member should fulfill his or her role in God's family.

In the biblical development of the theme of redemption, the conflict between the family of God and the family of Satan commences almost immediately after the Fall, culminates in the triumph of Jesus over sin and death "in the fullness of the time," and will be consummated when Jesus returns to judge the living and the dead on "the last day."[26] In the meantime, the antithesis of "children of God" and "children of the devil" continues to be the most significant factor of human history. Nobody can avoid being identified with either one family or the other. Those who are in Christ must

---

[24]1 Tim. 3:15.
[25]For example, read Matt. 12:46-50; 18:15-35; 23:8-10.
[26]See Gen. 3:15 and compare Gal. 4:4-6. Compare also Gen. 4:1-8 with 1 John 3:1-15.

perceive themselves as *members together* in the great *family of God.* That exalted relationship is implied by the term "brother," which is used repeatedly in the New Testament as an expression of Christian fellowship, and denotes an endeared one, a "near kinsman; in the plural, a community based on identity of origin or life."[27] If the word has an antonym in Paul's mind, it would not be "stranger," but "enemy":

> *If anyone does not obey our instruction in this letter, take special note of him. Do not associate with him, in order that he may feel ashamed. Yet do not regard him as an enemy, but warn him as a brother.*[28]

The apostle John also sees no middle ground in this matter of brotherhood: either we are actively involved in loving a brother by meeting his needs in the appropriate manner, or else we are hating our brother, and thus forfeit our right to be called children of God:

> *Anyone who hates his brother is a murderer, and you know that no murderer has eternal life in him....If anyone has material possessions and sees his brother in need but has no pity on him, how can the love of God be in him?*[29]

There is no social context in which love is demonstrated more fittingly, more tenderly, more patiently, more understandingly than in a *family relationship.* Even the world is said to "love its own."[30] How much more should we love

---

[27]W. E. Vine, *An Expository Dictionary of New Testament Words* (Westwood, NJ: Fleming H. Revell Co., 1965), pp. 154-155.
[28]2 Thess. 3:14-15. Of course, the Christian is to love even his enemies (Matt. 5:43-45; Rom. 12:7-18).
[29]1 John 3:15, 17. Compare 1 John 5:1ff.
[30]John 15:19.

one another, who understand the true nature of love and who share in a family heritage of eternal love?

The Same Father

Third, those who are members one of another in the same family also have the *same Father:*

> *Yet to all who received him, to those who believed in his name, he gave the right to become children of God—children born not of natural descent, nor of human decision or a husband's will, but born of God.*[31]

John says more about the new birth than any other New Testament writer. It is his favorite expression to describe the change of relationship to God that results from obedient faith in Jesus. Paul also refers to this transition in regenerative terms, but seems to prefer the legal categories of adoption and naturalization (change of citizenship). His Epistle to the Ephesians, which speaks predominantly of the church as the "body" of Christ, also contains several "family" references, among them the fatherhood of God:

> *For this reason I kneel before the Father, from whom his whole family in heaven and on earth derives its name....one God and Father of all, who is over all and through all and in all.*[32]

> *Be imitators of God, therefore, as dearly loved children and live a life of love, just as Christ loved us and gave himself up for us....*[33]

---

[31]John 1:12-13. Compare 1 Peter 1:3-4, 23-25.
[32]Eph. 3:14-15; 4:6.   [33]Eph. 5:1-2.

113

For Paul, the chief characteristic of the God who has been revealed in Christ is a self-sacrificing love toward others— particularly, toward the children of God. He calls on God's elect children to imitate this characteristic of their Father, who is the epitome of all true fatherhood and who shares His name with all whom He adopts "in Christ."

The Same Nature

Fourth, those who together wear the name of God are also made to partake of the *same nature:*

> *"Be perfect, therefore, as your heavenly Father is perfect."* [34]

> *But just as he who called you is holy, so be holy in all you do....* [35]

> *His divine power has given us everything we need for life and godliness through our knowledge of him who called us by his own glory and goodness. Through these he has given us his very great and precious promises, so that through them you may participate in the divine nature....* [36]

> *Therefore, if anyone is in Christ, he is a new creation; the old has gone, the new has come!* [37]

When conversion to Christ occurs, the reception of the Holy Spirit is realized and participation in the nature of God

---

[34]Matt. 5:48.   [35]1 Peter 1:15.   [36]2 Peter 1:3-4.
[37]2 Cor. 5:17. In this context, as in other Pauline discussions of "the new man," the concept is a *corporate* one,with social implications: a new *mankind,* characterized by Christlikeness in dealing with others (Eph. 2:14-16; 4:20-5:2; Col. 2:9-14).

114

begins. This is the point at which the obedient believer (as described above) is *justified,* but it is also the same moment at which he begins the growing process of *sanctification.* Nobody can be truly converted (initially) apart a fundamental change of heart in response to hearing and believing the Good News about God's redeeming love in Christ. This basic change of heart begins the life-long process of maturing, which causes the Christian to conform more and more to the likeness of Christ, who is the image of the invisible God.

The Same Likeness

Fifth, those who are "members one of another" are patterned after the *same likeness.* All true Christians are developing and maturing into "the full-grown image of Christ":

> *For those God foreknew he also predestined to be conformed to the likeness of his Son, that he might be the firstborn among many brothers.*[38]

> *In bringing many sons to glory, it was fitting that God, for whom and through whom everything exists, should make the author of their salvation perfect through suffering. Both the one who makes men holy and those who are made holy are of the same family. So Jesus is not ashamed to call them brothers....Since the children have flesh and blood, he too shared in their humanity so that by his death he might destroy him who holds the power of death—that is, the devil....For this reason he had to be made like his brothers in every way....*[39]

Jesus Christ is simultaneously the incarnation of God and the exaltation of man. He is the prototype of a new human-

[38]Rom. 8:29.
[39]Heb. 2:10-12, 14-15, 17. Compare also Rom. 8:3.

ity, living in unbroken fellowship with God. As Jesus embodies God and man dwelling together in unspoiled harmony and peace, so we who are in union with Him are destined also to embody this harmony of the human and the divine through His Spirit who dwells in us, sanctifies us, and will ultimately raise us to share in His own glorious immortality.[40]

The Same Promises

Sixth, those who are in Christ together are recipients of the *same promises:*

> *Peter replied, "Repent and be baptized, every one of you, in the name of Jesus Christ so that your sins may be forgiven. And you will receive the gift of the Holy Spirit. The promise is for you and your children and for all who are far off—for all whom the Lord our God will call."*[41]

> *You are all sons of God through faith in Christ Jesus, for all of you who were baptized into Christ have clothed yourselves with Christ. There is neither Jew nor Greek, slave nor free, male nor female, for you are all one in Christ Jesus. If you belong to Christ, then you are Abraham's seed, and heirs according to the promise.*[42]

The Same Inheritance

Throughout biblical history, one of the primary considerations of sonship has been heirship. The concept of "inheritance" plays a strategic role in the narratives concerning the

---

[40]See Phil. 3:20-21; 1 John 3:2.   [41]Acts 2:38-39.
[42]Gal. 3:26-29. The Abrahamic blessing involves the forgiveness of sins through the atoning death of the promised Seed (Christ), and the reception of the Spirit of sonship (Gal. 3:13-14).

promises of God to the Hebrew patriarchs. These promises were inherited by their descendants, not strictly on the basis of a direct line of physical descent, but because of God's purpose and plan. Hence, Isaac inherited the blessing, although Ishmael was older than he. The birthright fell to Jacob, but Esau had been first in order of birth. In later biblical history, the priesthood and the national throne would similarly pass from unworthy natural heirs (i.e., the houses of Eli and Saul, respectively) to those whom God chose to so bless.

In the New Testament, it is not those who pride themselves on being "in line" for divine blessing who are admitted by Jesus into the blessedness of the kingdom of God. It is rather the poor in spirit, the brokenhearted and the rejected, and those who do good to the needy brothers of Jesus who inherit the kingdom prepared for them before the foundation of the world. It is not the religious establishment of scribes and Pharisees who inherit forgiveness of sins and all of the glorious blessings which are betokened by the possession of the Spirit; it is the despised and persecuted community which gathers at the feet of the Nazarene who was crucified outside the gates of the holy city. It is not Abraham's blood that determines citizenship in the New Jerusalem, but rather the blood of Christ. All who trust in that blood are equally heirs of the *same inheritance:*

> *Now if we are children, then we are heirs—heirs of God and co-heirs with Christ, if indeed we share in his sufferings in order that we may also share in his glory.*[43]

---

[43]Rom. 8:17.

117

Praise be to the God and Father of our Lord Jesus Christ! In his great mercy he has given us new birth into a living hope through the resurrection of Jesus Christ from the dead, and into an inheritance that can never perish, spoil or fade—kept in heaven for you....In this you greatly rejoice, though now for a little while you may have had to suffer grief in all kinds of trials.[44]

This seventh shared reality (a heavenly *inheritance*) cannot be mentioned by Paul or by Peter without a reminder that the Spirit of life in Christ Jesus is also the Spirit of love, sacrifice, and denial of self. It is often painful to follow the Son of God through a sinful world, but the sufferings of this present time are only "for a little while," and are "not worth comparing with the glory that will be revealed in us."[45]

The Same Education

Eighth, all members of the body of Christ are students of the *same education*. Jesus was recognized as "the Teacher" long before He was proclaimed as "Lord." Even so, the second title can only strengthen the meaning of the first:

"You call Me 'Teacher' and 'Lord,' and rightly so, for that is what I am. Now that I, your Lord and Teacher, have washed your feet, you also should wash one another's feet."[46]

Discipleship to Christ is not optional for the Christian, but neither is it really possible apart from the objective revelation of Jesus found in Scripture. We must not attempt to

---

[44] 1 Peter 1:3-4, 6. The Epistle to the Hebrews has much to say about this "inheritance."
[45] Rom. 8:18. [46] John 13:13-14.

separate the incarnate Word from the written Word, either from the Old Testament (which promises a Messiah) or from the New Testament (which presents Jesus as the Christ). Our unity as "members one of another" is not the result of a common fondness for the sound of the name, "Jesus," but of a shared commitment to the *content* of that name:

> *"Now I commit you to God and to the word of his grace, which can build you up and give you an inheritance among all those who are sanctified."* [47]

> *But I am afraid that just as Eve was deceived by the serpent's cunning, your minds may somehow be led astray from your sincere and pure devotion to Christ. For if someone comes to you and preaches a Jesus other than the Jesus we preached, or if you receive a different spirit from the one you received, or a different gospel from the one you accepted, you put up with it easily enough.* [48]

The Same Discipline

A ninth trait that characterizes all who are "members one of another" in Christ is subjection to the *same discipline*. The writer of the Epistle to the Hebrews, having reminded his wavering readers of the steadfastness of their divine forerunner in His devotion to the Father's will and in His opposition to sin, makes this application to the spiritual brethren of Jesus:

---

[47] Acts 20:32.
[48] 2 Cor. 11:3-4. The unity of the Spirit is shared only among those who are trusting the "one Lord" who was manifested to, and proclaimed by, the apostles (1 Cor. 12:2-3; 1 John 1:1-4; 4:1-6; 2 John 7-11; 1 Tim. 3:16).

And you have forgotten that word of encouragement that addresses you as sons: "My son, do not make light of the Lord's discipline, and do not lose heart when he rebukes you, because the Lord disciplines those he loves, and he punishes everyone he accepts as a son." Endure hardship as discipline: God is treating you as sons. For what son is not disciplined by his father?...Our fathers disciplined us for a little while as they thought best; but God disciplines us for our good, that we may share in his holiness.[49]

The heavenly Father is an infallible disciplinarian, with regard to both method and motive. If the discipline of imperfect earthly fathers (whom Jesus described as "evil" in comparison to God)[50] was acknowledged as a benefit which brought future blessing, how then should Christians respond to the hardships through which their perfect heavenly Father molds their characters into conformity to His own? To share in the holiness of God is the "highest good" of any person, and while earthly parents often claim to love their children so much that they refuse to discipline them, our heavenly Father so loves His children that He will not refuse them any good thing—however painful for the moment.

The subject of "church discipline" may seem extremely distasteful to many Christians. A reluctant but obedient attitude toward this teaching is far preferable to the merry abandonment with which some have approached it. But as we study this subject, we should realize that if the local church refuses to obey the Father's command to discipline an ungodly person in its midst (one who is known as a

---

[49]Heb. 12:5-7, 10. See also Heb. 5:7-14; Rev. 3:19.
[50]See Matt. 7:11.

"brother" in the Lord), then that congregation cannot truthfully claim to love God, nor the Lord's church, nor that person whose soul is in jeopardy. The twofold purpose for disciplinary action in the local congregation by those who are "members one of another" is (1) the preservation of Christlike morality and purity in the local congregation and (2) the ultimate salvation of the unruly member.[51]

The Same Fruit

A tenth distinction of those who share in Christ as "members one of another" is the bearing of the *same fruit:*

> *But thanks be to God that, though you used to be slaves to sin, you wholeheartedly obeyed the form of teaching to which you were entrusted. You have been set free from sin and have become slaves to righteousness....When you were slaves to sin, you were free from the control of righteousness. What benefit did you reap at that time from the things you are now ashamed of? Those things result in death! But now that you have been set free from sin and have become slaves to God, the benefit you reap leads to holiness, and the result is eternal life....So, my brothers, you also died to the law through the body of Christ, that you might belong to another, to him who was raised from the dead, in order that we might bear fruit to God. For when we were controlled by the sinful nature, the sinful passions aroused by the law were at work in our bodies, so that we bore fruit for death.[52]*

> *But the fruit of the Spirit is love, joy, peace, patience, kind-*

---

[51]See 1 Cor. 5:1-8; James 5:19-20; 1 Tim. 1:18-20;
2 Thess. 3:14-15.
[52]Rom. 6:17, 20-22; 7:4-5.

ness, goodness, faithfulness, gentleness and self-control.
Against such things there is no law. Those who belong to
Christ Jesus have crucified the sinful nature with its passions
and desires.[53]

In the first divison of this book, I examined in some detail
the relationship between love, law, and legalism. My conclusion was that God's law may be followed out of a motive
of love for God and man, or out of a self-centered desire to
place God under legal obligation to oneself.[54]

Those who have wholeheartedly responded in obedience to
the gospel have been freely forgiven and have received the
Spirit of adoption in Christ. They are finished with pursuing
self-gratification and self-justification. Motivated by love
and gratitude rather than by fear and guilt, they are set free
to follow Jesus Christ without further self-concern. Such
people have willingly surrendered to God's decree that
"self" must die, and have deliberately picked up their own
crosses (executed the death sentence upon "self"), in order
that Christ might live in them. This spiritual union with
Jesus results in a life of undefiled love, balanced with compassionate righteousness. The spiritual fruit borne by those
who are in Christ is nothing other than the life of Jesus
being lived in and through them, by means of the Spirit
who dwells in them by faith.[55]

---

[53]Gal. 5:22-24.
[54]Part One, *The Love of Christ in the Local Congregation*, especially pp. 49-54.
[55]See John 15:1-8 and compare John 13:34-35.

The "Bottom Line"

What, then, do we share as "members one of another" in Christ's body, the church? What is our common heritage as those who are children in the family of God? At the bottom line, our heritage is God Himself. The Father of our Lord Jesus Christ has become *our Father*.[56] Together we share one Heavenly Father, one Divine Brother, and one Holy Spirit.[57] In Christ, God has freely chosen each one of us to be His own. In Christ, each one of us has freely chosen God to be "our God." In Christ, we have no choice except to choose one another; that is, to love, accept, and serve each brother and sister whom God has received in Christ.

---

[56]See John 20:17; Eph. 1:5-6.

[57]See Eph. 4:4-6. Paul's sevenfold statement concerning the unity of the Spirit should be considered neither reducible nor expandable in its requirements.

9

WHERE WE SHARE

Two analogies are repeatedly used throughout the New Testament to illustrate the meaning of the concept, "members one of another."[58] The "family" analogy is favored by the apostle John, and speaks of the intimacy and devotion of a *fraternal* relationship. Paul speaks of God's people primarily (though not exclusively) in terms of the "body" concept, a comparison which emphasizes the *functional* aspects of the "one another" relationship. In this chapter, I will focus attention mainly on the church as Christ's "body," drawing comments, conclusions, and applications from Paul's three classic texts concerning the "body" (1 Cor. 12:12-27; Rom. 12:1-8; Eph. 4:1-16).

---

[58]The body and family analogies overlap at certain points, but are nevertheless distinguishable. In affirming the importance of these two illustrations, I do not intend to deny the value of various other comparisons in the New Testament's presentation of God's people (e.g., a priesthood, a temple, a bride, etc.).

Background Of The "Body" Concept

How did Paul arrive at his concept of the church as "the body of Christ"? There are several possibilities. The idea may have been rooted in the Hebrew concept of corporate personality, in which one prominent name stands for the whole community under its headship. Some messianic portraits in the Old Testament Scriptures are characterized by this tight binding of God's people to their promised deliverer, and Paul could have applied the principle directly to Christ and the church.[59]

Perhaps, however, we should seek the origin of Paul's view of the church as Christ's "body" in his Damascus road encounter with the risen Christ:

> *"Who are you, Lord?" Saul asked. "I am Jesus, whom you are persecuting," he replied.*[60]

This identification of the glorified Christ with his persecuted disciples is later reflected in the language of Paul's Epistle to the Colossians, of which the headship of Christ is a prominent theme:

> *Now I rejoice in what was suffered for you, and I fill up in my flesh what is still lacking in regard to Christ's afflictions, for the sake of his body, which is the church.*[61]

Christ's "body" is the church, and Paul's sufferings on behalf of that body are a continuation of the afflictions of Christ.

Another possibility is that Paul's perception of the "body of

---

[59]See Isa. 53:1ff; Dan. 7:13-22, 27. [60]Acts 9:5. [61]Col. 1:24.

125

Christ" was derived from the words of Jesus on the night of His betrayal:

The Lord Jesus, on the night he was betrayed, took bread, and when he had given thanks, he broke it and said, "This is my body, which is for you...." [62]

And is not the bread that we break a participation in the body of Christ? Because there is one loaf, we, who are many, are one body, for we all partake of the one loaf. [63]

In the first Corinthian letter, there are close associations between the "one loaf" which *symbolizes* the body of Christ and the members who *comprise* the body of Christ, to the point that those Christians at Corinth who were inconsiderate of one another in the sharing of the covenant meal were

....guilty of sinning against the body and blood of the Lord....For anyone who eats and drinks without recognizing the body of the Lord [in context, the church—L.D.] *eats and drinks judgment on himself.* [64]

Any or all of the above factors may have contributed to Paul's understanding of the church as "the body of Christ." In the absence of any conclusive statement by Paul himself regarding the source of this analogy, we must be content to affirm that Paul's apostolic authority is from the Lord Jesus Christ, and that this authority ensures that whatever is verbalized or written by Paul in the Lord's name is truly from the mind of God. [65] With this understanding, we are ready to

---

[62]1 Cor. 11:23-24.   [63]1 Cor. 10:16-17.   [64]1 Cor. 11:27, 29.
[65]Dale Moody, *The Word of Truth* (Grand Rapids: Wm. B. Eerdmans Publ. Co., 1981), pp. 442-446. Paul made many claims of apostolic authority in his epistles, but none exceed the strength of those in the Corinthian letters (1 Cor. 2:6-13; 4:17; 4:21-5:5; 7:17, 40; 11:2, 17, 34; 14:36-38; 2 Cor. 10:8; 13:10).

consider the relevant passages from Paul.

The Nature Of The Body: A Unit Of God's Design

The body is a unit, though it is made up of many parts; and though all its parts are many, they form one body. So it is with Christ. For we were all baptized by one Spirit into one body— whether Jews or Greeks, slave or free—and we were all given the one Spirit to drink.

Now the body is not made up of one part but of many. If the foot should say, "Because I am not a hand, I do not belong to the body," it would not for that reason cease to be part of the body. And if the ear should say, "Because I am not an eye, I do not belong to the body," it would not for that reason cease to be part of the body. If the whole body were an eye, where would the sense of hearing be? If the whole body were an ear, where would the sense of smell be?

But in fact God has arranged the parts in the body, every one of them, just as he wanted them to be. If they were all one part, where would the body be? As it is, there are many parts, but one body. The eye cannot say to the hand, "I don't need you!" And the head cannot say to the feet, "I don't need you!" On the contrary, those parts of the body that seem to be weaker are indispensable, and the parts that we think are less honorable we treat with....special modesty, while our present-able parts need no special treatment.

But God has combined the members of the body and has given greater honor to the parts that lacked it, so that there should be no division in the body, but that its parts should have equal concern for each other. If one part suffers, every part suffers with it; if one part is honored, every part rejoices with it. Now you are the body of Christ, and each one of you is a part of it.[66]

---

[66] 1 Cor. 12:12-27.

The word "body" is the most prominent word in the structural unity of First Corinthians, and is therefore a hermeneutical key to the letter. It is used with reference to: individual believers in their conduct as persons united to Christ;[67] the collective church organism as composed of its individual members;[68] the substance of the incarnate Christ;[69] the manner of resurrection experienced by Christ and anticipated by those who are "in Him."[70] In the context of 1 Cor. 12, Paul is dealing with problems of disunity which have been occasioned by a misunderstanding of spiritual gifts and a misconception concerning the nature of the church. The "body" illustration is perfectly suited to express the proper perspectives and to lead into a discussion of the priority of love, which is the solution to all such problems.

Paul begins by reminding the gifted but carnal Corinthian congregation that all who have been baptized into Christ (including himself) share membership in the same body and are beneficiaries together of the same life-giving Spirit. From this point, he begins to employ the "body" analogy to vividly describe the *essential unity* that underlies the *necessary diversity* among the members of Christ's church:

> *Now the body is not made up of one part but of many....If the whole body were an eye, where would the sense of hearing be? If the whole body were an ear, where would the sense of*

[67]See 1 Cor. 6:13ff; 7:4, 34; 9:27.
[68]See 1 Cor. 10:17; 12:27.
[69]See 1 Cor. 10:16; 11:24.
[70]See 1 Cor. 15:1ff.

smell be? But in fact God has arranged the parts in the body, every one of them, just as he wanted them to be....The eye cannot say to the hand, "I don't need you!" And the head cannot say to the feet, "I don't need you!" [71]

The Body, The Individual, And God's Purpose

Christians have no guaranteed immunity from infection by the misconceptions and mythologies of their own time in history. In an age in which secular humanism, existentialism, and atheism dominate the arts and sciences, God's people desperately need to arm themselves with the mindset of revealed Christianity. History is going somewhere; man is not a cosmic accident; the living God is working out a purpose in the universe, and Christ is the Center of that purpose.

But there is more: God's purpose involves not only a Head, but also a body which, although distinct from the Head, is nevertheless inseparable from it. Every single member of that body has been personally chosen and placed into the body by God Himself, to function there according to its individual ability. There are no misfits, no accidents, no unplanned children in the family of God. There are no vestigial organs or useless members in the body of Christ. Each one is essential, each one is necessary, and all are interdependent in the proper functioning of the whole body. God's eternal purpose in Christ is the only sufficient answer to the individual's need for personal meaning, both vertically (in relationship to the Creator) and horizontally (in relationship to other human beings). We need Someone,

---

[71] 1 Cor. 12:14, 17-18, 21.

even as we need to be needed *by* someone. We are instinctively spiritual beings, having a compulsion to worship; yet, we are also naturally social creatures, needing meaningful relationships with those of our own kind. Secular humanism attempts to fulfill these human needs by spelling "man" with a capital "M" and urging everyone to rally around the human species as an object of worship. Meanwhile, God is inviting individual men and women to become His sons and daughters through the gospel of Jesus Christ, who has reconciled us to God and to one another by His cross.

Needed: A Change Of Perspective

Having glimpsed the greatness of the body of Christ in the eternal purpose of God, we must admit that it is easy for us to view the church and its members from a decidedly less exalted perspective. That eccentric old woman with the awful singing voice: is *she* really a part of God's eternal purpose? The downcast young man who always seems to be on the edge of a nervous breakdown: where does *he* fit into the body of Christ? And what about that recently converted welfare recipient who seems so morally insensitive and spiritually ignorant?

Paul says that each member has a place and a function in the eternally purposed body of Christ, but it is easy for the "more presentable" parts to despise those who seem "less honorable." The more showy parts of our bodies—the external, visible members such as the hands and face—receive a lot of our attention and care. We want to be sure that these members look good. But how much attention do we give to those vital, internal organs that are never seen? When was the last time you seriously considered your liver, your spleen, or your lungs? The secret of good physical health is to conscientiously care for these less glamorous, unseen parts. They are so important that, without them, the body ceases to function.

Certainly, some parts of our bodies are "inferior," from one point of view. I don't "need" my big toe in the same way I "need" my heart—but I still *need* that toe! My body won't function properly without it, and other parts will have to compensate for my big toe if it becomes injured or severed. And although I may not think about that toe even once during the course of an ordinary day, I will lavish attention upon it the moment I stub it. Every other member will then sympathize with that lowly digit, as its nerve endings relay the pain signal to the brain. The brain (head) will direct the body to take the weight from that toe, and the hand will use its unique abilities to soothe and caress the injured member.

The Corinthian church had a tendency to exalt the more showy gifts, such as tongues and prophecy, while downplaying those members whose gifts seemed less spectacular. So Paul painted this beautiful picture of Christ caring for the members of His body through their functioning as "members one of another" under His headship. But what Paul said to the Corinthians in this regard also has its meaning and application for today's local congregations. We must be concerned for the members who are "invisible," who are not out in front where their presence is obvious.

These members are not our great orators and teachers. They are not heads of committees; they do not lead the congregation in song. But what about the quiet, humble sister who goes about her business, instructing her children in the way of godliness, praying faithfully for those in the mission field, occasionally baking a pie for her neighbors next door, or opening her home to her brothers and sisters in Christ? We rarely hear anything about her, but she is doing a great work of faith. She is functioning as a member of the body; she is faithfully ministering according to the stewardship which the Lord has entrusted to her.

Some Are Evangelists, But All Are Evangelistic

We are too prone to exalt the seen above the unseen, the noisy above the quiet, the colorful above the bland. How often have Christian mission magazines and evangelical journals published feature articles on a hospitable Christian housewife or an exemplary Christian employee? We are often informed about how many conversions a given congregation has produced in the past year, but not a word is mentioned about the strength of its families, the quality of its fellowship, or the impact that its life-style is making on the surrounding community.

It seems that many Christians believe that the only people who are really involved in evangelism are "those who actually do the converting." Paul, while never denying the importance and necessity of baptizing people into Christ,[72] had a more balanced perspective on evangelism than most of us:

---

[72]See 1 Cor. 1:10-17. Paul was not discussing the importance or non-importance of baptism in this context, but rather the problem of division among the Corinthian Christians. He was thankful that someone else did most of the baptizing of the converts at Corinth, so that none of them could make a status symbol of being baptized by Paul, thus contributing to further division.

What, after all, is Apollos? And what is Paul? Only servants, through whom you came to believe—as the Lord has assigned to each his task. I planted the seed, Apollos watered it, but God made it grow. So neither he who plants nor he who waters is anything, but only God, who makes things grow. The man who plants and the man who waters have one purpose, and each will be rewarded according to his own labor.[73]

I have long been convinced that most souls are not won through the isolated efforts of any one individual. The Lord uses the lives of the many members of His body to bring people into a right relationship with Himself. Why then should we think only of the one who preaches or the one who baptizes as "a great soul-winner"? Because God gave only "some" to be *evangelists,* must we conclude that nobody else is *evangelistic?*

A friend of mine who is a gospel preacher tells of an evangelistic meeting in Florida where he had proclaimed the gospel of Christ. This preacher is a man of great magnetism and eloquence, and when he offered the audience an invitation to respond to the gospel, a certain man came forward to be baptized into Christ. The man had been considered the least likely candidate for Christianity of all who were there that night, one of those "unconvertible" types who could hardly be approached with the gospel at all. Everybody was praising the Lord because of this man's conversion. They were thrilled that this modern "Saul of Tarsus" was now a member of the body of Christ. Several of the local members gathered around the preacher. They were patting him on the back and saying, "What a powerful presentation! Did you see that response?"

---

[73] 1 Cor. 3:5-8.

My friend looked over the heads of his admirers, out beyond the doorway of the church building. Standing there alone in the yard, far removed from all the fanfare, stood the brother who had brought the man to the meeting in the first place. This *anonymous Christian* was as important in God's process of bringing that lost person to Jesus as my preacher-friend ever was. "The eye cannot say to the hand, 'I don't need you!'"

Every Member A Minister

Although only "some" in the church are entrusted with gifts of spiritual leadership, the goal toward which these gifts are to be applied in the body of Christ involves "all" the members:

> —to prepare God's people for works of service, so that the body of Christ may be built up until we all reach unity in the faith and in the knowledge of the Son of God and become mature, attaining to the whole measure of the fullness of Christ.[74]

The New Testament does not set forth a "clergy-laity" distinction. *God's people* are to do the works of service—that is, the *ministry*. There is no hint of an elite group that does the work while the rest remain spectators in the pews. Those who teach and lead are not a ruling class who are to be catered to and waited on by their "inferiors." On the contrary, they are to lead the way by serving their fellow members, thus equipping them to minister so that the whole body may grow together. The leaders among us are the

---

[74]Eph. 4:12-13.

servants, and the least is the greatest.

Do we doubt that our contribution to the growth of the body can amount to anything worthwhile? We should recall what Jesus was able to do with a meager offering of bread and fishes that was humbly and lovingly offered for His use. The God who manifested Himself in Christ is a God who takes little and makes much of it. The real question is whether or not we will surrender our "little lives" to Him so that He can make us what He wills, according to His eternal purpose in Christ.

> *Then we will no longer be infants, tossed back and forth by the waves, and blown here and there by every wind of teaching and by the cunning and craftiness of men in their deceitful scheming. Instead, speaking the truth in love, we will in all things grow up into him who is the Head, that is, Christ. From him the whole body, joined and held together by every supporting ligament, grows and builds itself up in love, as each part does its work.*[75]

Truth, Love, And Unity

Why should we help one another to reach unity and maturity in Christ? Why should we deny ourselves in order to serve one another in the body of Christ? It is so that none of the members of the body will linger on in the vulnerable state of spiritual infancy. Babyhood is the most helpless and unstable season of human life. The infant is completely at the mercy of the environment and the people around him. Particularly, there is the danger of the baby swallowing something that might harm or even kill him. Perhaps the

---

[75]Eph. 4:14-16.

135

baby will not receive enough to eat, as in many third world nations where the infant mortality rate is so terribly high. The first year of life is a critical time, no less in the second birth than in the first. The process of growing, developing, and maturing in Jesus will keep us from losing our lives to the poisonous opinions of men.

The world is at least as full of deception today as it was in the first century. The worship of graven images has given way to pragmatic materialism, liberal theology, and naturalistic philosophy. But idol worship is still idol worship, whether practiced in ancient or modern forms. All false doctrines contain a smattering of truth which makes them *sound* good. Nevertheless, there is a specific body of teaching in the Bible that is called "the truth," and it is not open to negotiation:

> *We did not give in to them for a moment, so that the truth of the gospel might remain with you.*[76]

Unity at the expense of truth ceases to be Christianity, and becomes a corrupt compromise. Likewise, a strong doctrinal stand on "truth" at the expense of compassion and love is a perversion of Christianity. *To leave love is to lose unity.* It is possible for people to intellectually agree on the seven absolutes of Christian unity—one body, one Spirit, one hope, one Lord, one faith, one baptism, one God and Father—and still fail to please the Lord:

> *"I know your deeds, your hard work and your perseverance. I know that you cannot tolerate wicked men, that you have*

---

[76]Gal. 2:5.

tested those who claim to be apostles but are not, and have found them false. You have persevered and endured hardships for my name, and have not grown weary. Yet I hold this against you: You have forsaken your first love. Remember the height from which you have fallen! Repent and do the things you did at first. If you do not repent, I will come to you and remove your lampstand from its place." [77]

There are congregations today that give intellectual assent to the absolutes of unity; they make sure that all their functioning is correct in its form. But there is no life in them, because there is no love there. If we do not have love as the basis and means of our unity, we have only something cold and formal. We may have no dissension in our ranks and everything may be neat and orderly, but if we think that these things alone are sufficient, let us remember that most funeral parlors can boast of these same qualities! The unity that promotes growth to maturity thrives on a loving, dynamic, healthy interaction among members of the body of Christ:

> *Instead, speaking the truth in love, we will in all things grow up into him who is the Head, that is, Christ. From him the whole body, joined and held together by every supporting ligament, grows and builds itself up in love, as each part does its work.* [78]

Unity On Purpose

The unity of the Spirit which binds a Christian community together as it grows toward maturity is something that must be purposely and actively maintained. Unity was not

---

[77]Rev. 2:2-5.
[78]Eph. 4:15-16.

formed by chance or accident, nor will it be preserved without definite intent and determination. We entered the unity of the Spirit when, in response to the gospel of Christ, we deposed "Lord Self" and enthroned Jesus as Lord of our lives. If unity is to be preserved at the level of the local church, each member must maintain a personal commitment to Jesus as Lord of his or her life and Head of His body. Our personal preferences, tastes, and conveniences must consistently give way to the Lord's desire that His people use their talents and resources to help one another toward spiritual maturity.

"Just As I Am"—Or Else!

> For by the grace given to me I say to every one of you: Do not think of yourself more highly than you ought, but rather think of yourself with sober judgment, in accordance with the measure of faith God has given you. Just as each of us has one body with many members, and these members do not all have the same function, so in Christ we who are many form one body, and each member belongs to all the others. We have different gifts, according to the grace given us. If a man's gift is prophesying, let him use it in proportion to his faith. If it is serving, let him serve; if it is teaching, let him teach; if it is encouraging, let him encourage; if it is contributing to the needs of others, let him give generously; if it is leadership, let him govern diligently; if it is showing mercy, let him do it cheerfully.[79]

This passage contains the New Testament's most explicit definition of the "members one of another" concept: "Each member belongs to all the others." This idea of individuals submitting to one another and belonging to each other in

---

[79]Rom. 12:3-8.

one body under one Head is a *covenant* concept which finds its most intimate expression in the marriage relationship:

> *"Haven't you read," he replied. "that at the beginning the Creator 'made them male and female,' and said, 'For this reason a man will leave his father and mother and be united to his wife, and the two will become one flesh'? So they are no longer two, but one. Therefore what God has joined together, let man not separate."* [80]

> *The wife's body does not belong to her alone but also to her husband. In the same way, the husband's body does not belong to him alone but also to his wife.* [81]

> *Submit to one another out of reverence for Christ. Wives, submit to your husbands as to the Lord. For the husband is the head of the wife as Christ is the head of the church, his body, of which he is the Savior.* [82]

The *covenant concept* is the juncture at which the *family* and *body* analogies meet: members of both types of unit *belong to one another* by virtue of their relationship of submission under one head. A detailed consideration of the family analogy will be taken up in a later chapter; our present concern is the diversity of talents and stewardships within the one body of Christ.

In Romans 12, Paul begins to exhort the Christians at Rome to live their lives in response to the mercies of God, which he had extolled at the conclusion of Romans 11. He urges them to offer themselves wholly to God in a life of continual worship. In order to render this acceptable service, these Christians will need to replace worldly thought patterns

---

[80]Matt. 19:4-6.   [81]1 Cor. 7:4.   [82]Eph. 5:21-23.

with godly ones. Paul's discussion of humble service and diversity in the one body of Christ immediately follows his admonition to be "transformed by the renewing of your mind." The flow of the context indicates that *humble acceptance of diversity among members of Christ's one body is a specific category of thought in which our minds need renewal.* Each one of us tends to think that everyone else should be "Just As I Am"!

Will The Real Unity Please Stand Up?

Many Christians entertain worldly concepts of "unity." Some mistakenly believe that unity is an authoritarian *unanimity,* in which somebody applies pressure in order to obtain absolute conformity; a rubber stamp *uniformity,* where there is a complete similarity of organization, external appearance, or method among many entities. Another popular misconception of unity among Christians equates Christian unity with ecumenical *union,* which is merely political affiliation, and doesn't necessarily include personal agreement among the participants. All the while, true Christian unity remains unknown, or at least unrecognized, by those whose ideas of unity cannot be reconciled with Paul's: various kinds of people can help one another toward maturity by employing their unique ministries in serving one another under one Head. Biblical unity is neither the "agreement to disagree," nor the "rubber stamp syndrome." It is oneness of heart and agreement in essential purpose through possession of the same life:

> *"My prayer is not for them alone. I pray also for those who will believe in me through their message, that all of them may be one, Father, just as you are in me and I am in you. May*

they also be in us so that the world may believe that you have sent me."[83]

May the God who gives endurance and encouragement give you a spirit of unity among yourselves as you follow Christ Jesus, so that with one heart and mouth you may glorify the God and Father of our Lord Jesus Christ. Accept one another, then, just as Christ accepted you, in order to bring praise to God.[84]

I appeal to you, brothers, in the name of our Lord Jesus Christ, that all of you agree with one another so that there may be no divisions among you and that you may be perfectly united in mind and thought. My brothers, some from Chloe's household have informed me that there are quarrels among you. What I mean is this: One of you says, "I follow Paul"; another, "I follow Apollos"; another, "I follow Cephas"; still another, "I follow Christ." Is Christ divided? Was Paul crucified for you? Were you baptized into the name of Paul?[85]

If you have any encouragement from being united with Christ, if any comfort from his love, if any fellowship with the Spirit, if any tenderness and compassion, then make my joy complete by being like-minded, having the same love, being one in spirit and purpose. Do nothing out of selfish ambition or vain conceit, but in humility consider others better than yourselves. Each of you should look not only to your own interests, but also to the interests of others. Your attitude should be the same as that of Christ Jesus....[86]

The themes of biblical unity are few, but frequently cited: a common life, a shared purpose, humble service, mutual acceptance, brotherly consideration. The New Testament repeatedly calls us back to "the mind of Christ": a genuinely humble self-concept, balanced with a healthy self-

---

[83]John 17:20-21.   [84]Rom. 15:5-7.
[85]1 Cor. 1:10-13.   [86]Phil. 2:1-5.

esteem, from which love pours forth in the form of practical service toward others.

Jesus walked this earth as deity incarnate, but He did not forget His submission to, and dependence on, His heavenly Father in fulfilling His redemptive mission. He refused to think of Himself more highly than He ought; the devil's temptations to do so only reinforced His faithfulness to the Father. The "one mind" we are to share is that of Christ Himself. The "one body" is that realm in which we live this new life together.

10

WHY WE SHARE

*Why is it that [God] gives us these special abilities to do
certain things best? It is that God's people will be equipped to
do better work for Him, building up the church, the body of
Christ, to a position of strength and maturity; until finally we
all believe alike about our salvation and about our Savior,
God's Son, and all become full-grown in the Lord—yes, to the
point of being filled full with Christ.*

*Then we will no longer be like children, forever changing our
minds about what we believe because someone has told us
something different, or has cleverly lied to us and made the
lie sound like the truth. Instead we will lovingly follow the
truth at all times—speaking truly, dealing truly, living truly—
and so become more and more in every way like Christ who is
the Head of His body, the church. Under His direction the
whole body is fitted together perfectly, and each part in its
own special way helps the other parts, so that the whole body
is healthy and growing and full of love.*[87]

---

[87]Eph. 4:12-16, *Living Bible: Paraphrased* (Wheaton, IL: Tyndale
House Publ., 1971).

Paul's explanation of the reason for the leadership gifts in the church is expressed in terms of the growth of a body— the body of Christ—to a state of maturity. This state of maturity was the goal that Christ had in mind for His body when He gave "some to be apostles, some to be prophets, some to be evangelists, and some to be pastors and teachers" in the church. A body cannot be more mature than its individual members, but neither do its members grow apart from the body. The body is designed to grow as a *unit*. Certain parts of one's physical body may reach maturity more rapidly than others. The feet, for example, may reach their full size long before one's whole stature has been attained. However, the goal is not merely "big feet" (or a big mouth!); it is a *mature body*.

The Goal Of God's Call

Although the newborn Christian is as forgiven, as justified, and as saved as anyone can possibly be, he is still far from the goal of spiritual maturity. Christ, it has been said, did not come to earth merely in order to get us into heaven; He came also to get heaven into us! The person who obeys the gospel and is added to the body of Christ is not finished with the spiritual quest; indeed, he has hardly begun! There is far more to anticipate in Christ than simply "dying and going to heaven." God wants to re-create us in His own unspoiled image, in the likeness of His Son, Jesus Christ. God, in Christ, took on our human nature so that we might put on His own divine nature:

> —*until we all attain unity in the faith and in the knowledge of the Son of God and become mature, attaining to the whole*

measure of the fullness of Christ.... You were taught, with regard to your former way of life, to put off your old self, which is being corrupted by its deceitful desires; to be made new in the attitude of your minds; and to put on the new self, created to be like God in true righteousness and holiness.[88]

The Meaning Of Maturity

Maturity is a concept that must be defined in terms of the specific discipline or goal to which it is applied. A "mature" musician would possess certain characteristics not necessarily found in the "mature" woodsman. The discipline of Christianity looks toward the goal of a community of Christlike members. Paul viewed Christ's life as the embodiment of full humanness:

—until we all arrive at the unity of the faith and of the full knowledge of the Son of God, at a complete man, at the measure of the fullness of Christ....[89]

The goal of Christian discipleship, then, is nothing less than "a complete man"—the fulfillment of all that God designed us to be. Christianity is not "religion," in the modern sense of the word; it is not a set of abstract propositions and principles that never touch the ground. It is not a list of prohibitions and techniques that diminishes our involvement in the world and narrows our outlook on life. Christianity broadens and enhances our humanity. It completes what is lacking in our humanness.

---

[88]Eph. 4:13, 22-24.
[89]Eph. 4:13, based on Alfred Marshall's *The Nestle Greek Text with a Literal Translation* (London: Samuel Bagster & Sons Ltd., 1958), p. 642.

Whatever is inherently *human* is also inherently *Christian*, including the full enjoyment and expression of the arts, science, gainful employment, recreation, sexuality, sports, and other so-called "secular" concerns. Sin is the only characteristic of humanity that is not natively Christian, but neither is it natively human: the life of Jesus of Nazareth has exposed sin for the intruder that it is. Sin has no business in our lives because it had no place in His. So Christian discipleship is an education in how to be whole men and women. Jesus is the Teacher, the world is the classroom, each local church is the student body, and the course lasts a lifetime.

What We Need To Learn

We need to learn to love. In the preceding section entitled *The Love Of Christ In The Local Congregation,* I devoted much space to explaining the uniqueness of the love of Christ. It is not a love that is "natural" with any of us. Even Christ Himself in His humanity had to deliberately *choose* this life principle—not only once or twice, but in His moment by moment living, and in His dying. He put on humanity *for others;* He washed dirty feet *for others;* He poured out His life *for others.* If fallen man has any natural instinct, it is the drive to live for himself instead of for God and for others.

Yet, man was created in the image of God in order that he might love God with his whole heart, soul, mind and strength, and love his neighbor as himself. Our chosen self-centeredness and self-assertiveness have produced this present wasteland of broken relationships, human exploitation

146

and abuse, oppression, crime, and warfare. There can be no literal return to Eden, but we are still confronted with a choice between the tree of life and the tree of the knowledge of good and evil: the cross of Christ or the assertion of self. If we choose the way of the cross, we find ourselves in the body of Christ, but not yet in an unspoiled Paradise. This is why the Bible says so much about the importance of Christians loving one another: all problems in human relationships can be handled if each of us is willing to refuse the rule of self and embrace the rule of love.

Loving Spirit, Living Body

Although the functioning of Christians as "members one of another" is best expressed in terms of the *body* concept, the inner spirit and motivation of that relationship is most vividly depicted by the *family* analogy. In Romans 12, Paul follows up on his exhortation to the Christian community as a "body" by describing the character of the Christian heart. He begins with a call for genuine love:

> *Love must be sincere. Hate what is evil; cling to what is good. Be devoted to one another in brotherly love. Honor one another above yourselves.*[90]

Without a loving spirit, the body has no life. The Spirit of God, through Paul, breathes life into the body concept by calling for a love that seeks the good and shuns the evil, honors the brother above oneself, serves the Lord zealously, perseveres joyfully, prays patiently, practices hospitality, blesses persecutors, lives harmoniously and humbly, and

---

[90]Rom. 12:9-10.

refuses to "play God" in the matter of avenging personal offenses. The "sincere" love described by Paul in Romans 12:9-21 is the love of Christ Himself. Paul here outlines the life-style of a community (body) that is walking in this love. Many of the exhortations in this section are echoes of Christ's own commands,[91] and the embodiment of these teachings by Jesus is obvious to anyone who reads the gospel accounts of His life.

"Friendly Love Of Kindred"

Among the first aspects of the love of Christ that Paul sets forth in this section is "brotherly love" (*philadelphia*): the quality of love that exists among members of the same family.[92] Paul's exhortation, as literally translated from the Greek text, reads:

> —*in brotherly love to one another loving warmly....*[93]

The adverbial expression "loving warmly" is a Greek compound word, *philostorgos*. Its literal meaning is "friendly love of kindred." It occurs only here in the New Testament, although the negative form *astorgos* (translated "without

---

[91]Compare, for example: Rom. 12:13 with Matt. 5:42; Rom. 12:14 with Matt. 5:44; Rom. 12:17, 19 with Matt. 5:39.

[92]The depiction of the Christian community as a family is a prominent theme in the New Testament. Jesus Himself spoke of His disciples in such terms (see Matt. 12:46-50; 18:15-35; 23:8; 25:40; John 20:17; 1 Tim. 3:15; Heb. 2:11-15; 1 John 3:1-10).

[93]Rom. 12:10, from Alfred Marshall, *The Nestle Greek Text with a Literal English Translation* (London: Samuel Bagster & Sons Ltd., 1958), p. 642.

natural affection") occurs in two other places.[94]

In the first-century Roman world, it was customary for a mother's maidservant to lay the newborn child before its father. If the Roman father picked up the child and held it in his hands, it meant that he received and accepted the baby as his own; if he turned around and walked away, the infant would be abandoned to die of exposure. Paul undoubtedly referred to practices of this type when he described many of his contemporaries as being *astorgos*: "without natural affection." It is *natural* for parents to love and accept their own children.

We live in a time when respect for human life is at a low ebb, when many parents are refusing to receive their own children. We witness the onslaught of violent, destructive forces against the family unit in modern society. Selfishness and greed are consuming our society because so many people are "looking out for number one," concerned only with pleasing themselves. Selfishness can pervert and destroy even "natural affection"; it can tear families apart and cause parents to kill their own children, and children their own parents. In glaring contrast to the ugly lack of natural affection that was steadily destroying the culture of ancient Rome (as it is our own), Paul expects the people of God to shine forth as the family of God. Christians are to be warm, tender, hospitable, and kind toward one another because they are members of the same family. If the body analogy describes the relationship of "members one of another" from a *functional* perspective, it is the family unit that best

---

[94]The NIV translates the negative form "heartless" (Rom. 1:31) and "without love" (2 Tim. 3:3).

149

illustrates the *psychological* aspects of that relationship. It is not that God's spiritual family is "something like" our earthly family units; it is rather that our earthly families are types or models of God's eternally purposed family in Christ. Members of the family of God are bound together by a "blood brotherhood" that transcends time and space:

> *For he chose us in him before the creation of the world to be holy and blameless in his sight.... In him we have redemption through his blood, the forgiveness of sins, in accordance with the riches of God's grace....*[95]

> *For you know that it was not with perishable things such as silver or gold that you were redeemed from the empty way of life handed down to you from your forefathers, but with the precious blood of Christ, a lamb without blemish or defect. He was chosen before the creation of the world, but was revealed in these last times for your sake.*[96]

Life In God's "Forever" Family

Relationships in this "forever family" should be even more cohesive and more intimate in the sharing of life's joys and sufferings than blood ties that are only biological:

> *Then Jesus' mother and brothers arrived. Standing outside, they sent someone in to call him. A crowd was sitting around him, and they told him, "Your mother and brothers are outside looking for you." "Who are my mother and my brothers?" He asked. Then he looked at those seated in a circle around him and said, "Here are my mother and my brothers! Whoever does God's will is my brother and sister and mother."*[97]

---

[95]Eph. 1:4, 7.   [96]1 Peter 1:18-20.
[97]Mark 3:31-35. Compare Matt. 12:46-50; Luke 11:27-28.

He came to that which was his own, but his own did not receive him. Yet to all who received him, to those who believed in his name, he gave the right to become children of God—children born not of natural descent, nor of human decision or a husband's will, but born of God.[98]

Now that you have purified yourselves by obeying the truth so that you have sincere love for your brothers, love one another deeply, from the heart. For you have been born again, not of perishable seed, but of imperishable, through the living and enduring word of God.[99]

In Jesus, we are a *family unit;* the "one new man" in Christ encompasses believers from all the families of the earth. The cross of Christ has succeeded where the tower of Babel has failed, for the unity of the human family must be built on God's foundation, not man's. There can be no true family of man unless it is the family of God.

Paul's admonition to the Christians of Rome concerning "brotherly love" calls for two qualities that capture the essence of what family life is all about. First, he calls for deliberate *devotion*:

Be devoted to one another in brotherly love. Honor one another above yourselves.[100]

Second, Paul enjoins a deep sharing of *emotion:*

Rejoice with those who rejoice; mourn with those who mourn.[101]

---

[98]John 1:11-13. [99]1 Peter 1:22-23.
[100]Rom. 12:10. [101]Rom. 12:15.

151

Even though brotherly love is natural among brothers, it isn't something that automatically happens among the members of a family. It must be deliberately, consistently cultivated and applied. This is even more the case in the family of God, since ours is not a "natural" family, but a *super*natural one.

We are "born from above" by the same Spirit into the one family, but we're not experienced at seeing one another from this heavenly perspective. Therefore, the New Testament writers repeatedly command and exhort Christians to love one another as brothers—that is, devotedly and emotionally.[102] This emphasis in the New Testament implies that each of us has a personal responsibility before the Lord to honestly examine his or her attitudes and actions toward all the brothers and sisters in God's family, and particularly toward those who are members with us in the local congregation:

> *Be devoted to one another in brotherly love. Honor one another above yourselves.... Share with God's people who are in need. Practice hospitality.... Rejoice with those who rejoice; mourn with those who mourn. Live in harmony with one another. Do not be proud, but be willing to associate with people of low position. Do not be conceited.*[103]

Christians must ask themselves how they are doing in this matter of brotherly love. For example, am I taking the initiative in showing honor to my brothers and sisters, or do I honor only those who honor me? Do I share generously with any needy Christian, or do I give only what I wish to

---

[102]See, for example, 1 Thess. 4:9; 1 Peter 1:22; 2 Peter 1:7; Heb. 13:1 (Greek text).   [103]Rom. 12:10, 13, 15-16.

give, whenever I happen to feel like giving, and to whomever I wish to give? Am I willing to share in the joys and sorrows of any brother or sister who is part of the family of God, or do I carefully restrict my concern and involvement to the lives of a certain "chosen few"— the few *I* choose?

Of course, it is neither possible nor desirable for every member of a local church to share in every other member's affairs to an equal degree. Paul, for instance, expected Christians to please God by caring for the needs of their own relatives, "so that the church can help those widows who are really in need."[104] Nevertheless, there is to be a mutual understanding among local church members that, as brothers and sisters in God's family who have entered into covenant with God and with one another, their lives and property are at one another's disposal, as real needs arise:

> *All the believers were one in heart and mind. No one claimed that any of his possessions was his own, but they shared everything they had....There were no needy persons among them.*[105]

It is time for today's Christians to stop regarding the first-century church as a quaint, historical curiosity that happened "once upon a time, in a land far away." The historical circumstances of the church have indeed changed, and any attempt to understand and reproduce first-century Christianity in our modern world is doomed to fail unless such changes are taken into account.

---

[104]1 Tim. 5:16. See also 1 Tim. 5:3-8.
[105]Acts 4:32, 34.

But men and women have not changed. Human beings are constitutionally the same today as they were in the days of the apostles. The Spirit of true community that made the church of the first century such an attractive and powerful phenomenon in that era is something that can be restored and must be taken seriously.

In our age of psychoanalysis, "self-help" seminars, secular support groups, fragmented families, and welfare programs, it is not hard to list many things that the church represented to earlier eras that it no longer represents to our own. Perhaps we have surrendered too much sacred ground to secular organizations. We have retreated from the real world of human needs and problems into a wasteland of irrelevant "religious" concerns. While our world stumbles in spiritual darkness and starves for lack of living bread, we debate "church issues" among ourselves.

The world is a big orphanage, under the tyranny of a cruel headmaster named Satan. Outside of Christ, there is no loving Father, no true brotherhood, no secure home. The biblical emphasis on the church as *God's family* is as relevant and appealing today as it was in apostolic times. But we must offer more than *doctrines* about the church as "family"; we must demonstrate the *reality* of family in our day by day living in the world.

Honest Evaluation

We must honestly evaluate our true attitudes toward one another as brothers and sisters in Christ, as members of the same family. Are we sensitive and responsive to one another's joys and sorrows, or are we indifferent and apathetic? If tension, hostility, or cold indifference characterize our attitude toward one another, we forfeit our place in God's family. We remove ourselves from the shelter and security of God's covenant love. We no longer have title to the blessings that God has graciously committed to His children:

> *"Therefore, if you are offering your gift at the altar and there remember that your brother has something against you, leave your gift there in front of the altar. First go and be reconciled to your brother; then come and offer your gift. Settle matters quickly with your adversary who is taking you to court. Do it while you are still with him on the way, or he may hand you over to the judge...."* [106]

We must not be indifferent about our brother's feelings toward us. The first move is always ours in settling grievances with a brother. The stakes are too high to justify any delay on our part, for the issue is the acceptability of our lives before the judge of all mankind. If our whole life in Christ is to be regarded as divine worship, as the New Testament clearly teaches, then we cannot live acceptably before God while we are content to continue in an unsettled relationship with our brother. We must pursue a right relationship with our brother so that we can continue to offer ourselves to God as "living sacrifices."

Jesus also anticipated the case of the disciple whose brother has sinned against him: he is to make every possible effort to bring the brother to repentance and reconciliation, but if all else fails, the impenitent offender is no longer to be regarded as a family member. Ideally, the offender and his

---

[106]Matt. 5:23-25.

offended brother would meet one another half way, as each went forth to seek peace with the other:

> *"If your brother sins against you, go and show him his fault, just between the two of you. If he listens to you, you have won your brother over. But if he will not listen, take one or two others along, so that 'every matter may be established by the testimony of two or three witnesses.' If he refuses to listen to them, tell it to the church; and if he refuses to listen even to the church, treat him as you would a pagan or a tax collector."* [107]

Deep Feelings

Brotherly love will always seek to make peace within the family, and to work out interpersonal problems with a brother or sister. It will do so, not merely because it is "right" to be in proper relationship with our brothers and sisters, but because *it hurts so much when our relationship with one another is not what it should be.* Brotherly love involves deep feelings toward one's fellow family members, feelings which grow as we come to know one another and become more intimately involved in one another's lives. However, human beings are capable of certain "deep feelings" that can actually prohibit our intimate involvement in one another's lives, and have nothing in common with brotherly love.

For example, I heard of a congregation in which two men continued to see one another in the worship assembly week after week, but refused to speak at all to one another. This went on for about fifteen years! A new preacher was even-

---

[107]Matt. 18:15-17.

tually hired, who soon became aware of this "dumb" dispute and called the two men into his office to resolve the situation. "What in the world could have caused such a deep estrangement between you two men?" the preacher inquired. Neither man could really remember what had originally caused the rift between them, and yet they hadn't spoken to one another in a decade and a half! Apparently, these men never seriously considered the commandment of Jesus: "Settle matters quickly with your adversary...." They had feelings toward one another that ran deeper than their memories could penetrate, but these feelings had nothing to do with brotherly love. Brotherly love is a loyal devotion which leads to deep emotion. "Where your treasure is, there your heart will be also."

When a Christian becomes frustrated or hurt by the thoughtless or offensive behavior of another Christian, there is usually a strong temptation to quietly withdraw from the relationship. It would probably be easier to crawl into a private corner for some emotional and psychological wound-licking than to deliberately confront the source of one's pain. Aware of our weakness, Jesus forbids us the deadly luxury of complacency in this matter. Whether we are offended by a brother or whether a brother takes offense concerning us, Jesus (in effect) says, "The ball is in your court. Go and be reconciled to your brother."

"But I Don't Feel Like It!"

If we are honest with ourselves, we must admit that we don't always *feel* like doing what the Lord commands us to do. There may be good reasons why we lack the *feelings*

157

that we believe should motivate us to be involved in sharing the joys, the sorrows, and even the frustrating idiosyncrasies of one another's lives. We must examine ourselves to determine the reasons for our lack of feelings toward our brothers and sisters in Christ, for the problem can become serious enough to separate us from God, unless it is properly diagnosed and treated.[108]

One obvious rationale for noninvolvement in the lives of others is *fear of rejection.* A child quickly learns to avoid the painful experience of getting burned by suppressing the instinct to touch. Many people who have experienced particularly intense or frequent emotional "burns" in the form of harsh criticisms of their personalities or accomplishments choose to cope with this pain by detachment from others. A popular songwriter captured this mindset brilliantly in a lyric that reveals a heart, cut deeply and frequently, now a massive callous of cynicism:

> I have no need of friendship; friendship causes pain. Its laughter and its loving I disdain. I am a rock, I am an island....And a rock feels no pain. And an island never cries.[109]

---

[108]For example, the apostle John wrote: "Anyone who does not love remains in death. Anyone who hates his brother is a murderer, and you know that no murderer has eternal life in him....If anyone has material possessions and sees his brother in need but has no pity on him, how can the love of God be in him?" (1 John 3:14-15, 17). John equates indifference and nonresponsiveness toward the problems of our fellow-Christians with a lack of love, which amounts to hatred and murder. The phrase, "has no pity on him" is literally, "shuts up his bowels from him." This Jewish idiom speaks not only of the withholding of benefits, but also of the suppression of deep feelings.

[109]Paul Simon's song, "I Am a Rock."

Rejection hurts—there is no point in denying that, but there is no need to become a "rock"! Rejection hurt Jesus to the point of death. But, thanks be to God, Jesus didn't respond to the pain by ending His involvement with the human race. Because of His great love for His heavenly Father and for His human brothers and sisters, He bore the pain of our rejection in His own body, and entrusted the outcome to God. Peter urged Christians to handle their own undeserved injuries in the same way:

> ...Christ suffered for you, leaving you an example, that you should follow in his steps. "He committed no sin, and no deceit was found in his mouth." When they hurled their insults at him, he did not retaliate; when he suffered, he made no threats. Instead, he entrusted himself to him who judges justly.[110]

Emotional insensitivity and lack of concerned involvement in the lives of others may be rooted in the *poverty of emotional expression* in one's own family background. Many children grow up in environments where love and affection are unknown, much less openly displayed. A child who never hears "I love you," who never basks in the tenderness of another's heartfelt affection,will find it most difficult to express love in the family of God in later life. He may have been baptized; she may know the forgiving grace of God's love in her life. But the emotional damage resulting from years of negligence, psychological abuse, and "negative programming" could take more than a lifetime to completely overcome. This is one of the most tragic illustrations of the biblical principle that sinful ways (and their consequences) are often passed from one generation to the next:

---

[110]1 Peter 2:21-23.

"He will by no means leave the guilty unpunished, visiting the iniquity of fathers on the children and on the grandchildren to the third and fourth generations." [111]

On the other hand, many people in modern western society are growing up in an atmosphere of moral laxity, permissiveness, indulgence, and irresponsibility. The popularity of concepts such as commitment, covenant, loyalty, and responsibility has plummeted in recent years. The "me decade" of the seventies has given way to an unabashed *pursuit of self-centered concerns,* usually in the form of career, material affluence, physical fitness, and cosmetic attractiveness. As Israel was enticed by the Baal worship surrounding her, so the Christian is not above the temptation to sacrifice his or her most precious relationships and responsibilities on the altar of the modern "cult of self-worship":

Do not love the world or anything in the world. If anyone loves the world, the love of the Father is not in him. For everything in the world—the cravings of sinful man, the lust of his eyes and the boasting of what he has and does—comes not from the Father but from the world....If anyone has material possessions and sees his brother in need but has no pity on him, how can the love of God be in him?[112]

What good is it, my brothers, if a man claims to have faith but has no deeds? Can such faith save him? Suppose a brother or sister is without clothes and daily food. If one of you says to him, "Go, I wish you well; keep warm and well fed," but does nothing about his physical needs, what good is it?...When you ask, you do not receive, because you ask with wrong motives, that you may spend what you get on your pleasures. You

---

[111]Exod. 34:7 (New American Standard Version).
[112]1 John 2:15-16; 3:17.

adulterous people, don't you know that friendship with the world is hatred toward God?[113]

The reality of our Christian love and faith is demonstrated when members of God's family are compassionately involved in meeting one another's needs. The essence of genuine Christian experience is a moment by moment repudiation of "self," with a corresponding response to Christ as Lord. To love and serve one another is His command, and in doing good to one another we are rightly serving Christ. To selfishly despise a brother in his hour of need is to be guilty of the most basic form of unfaithfulness to our covenant relationship with God in Christ. Covenant faithfulness in Christ is primarily a matter of spontaneously loving one another:

> *"Give to the one who asks you, and do not turn away from the one who wants to borrow from you....No one can serve two masters. Either he will hate the one and love the other, or he will be devoted to the one and despise the other. You cannot serve both God and Money."* [114]

> *"Then the righteous will answer him, 'Lord, when did we see you hungry and feed you, or thirsty and give you something to drink? When did we see you a stranger and invite you in, or needing clothes and clothe you? When did we see you sick or in prison and go to visit you?' The King will reply, 'I tell you the truth, whatever you did for one of the least of these brothers of mine, you did for me.'"* [115]

> *Keep on loving each other as brothers. Do not forget to entertain strangers, for by so doing some people have entertained angels without knowing it. Remember those in prison*

[113]James 2:14-16; 4:3-4.   [114]Matt. 5:42; 6:24.
[115]Matt. 25:37-40.

161

as if you were their fellow prisoners, and those who are mistreated as if you yourselves were suffering....And do not forget to do good and to share with others, for with such sacrifices God is pleased.[116]

We must act immediately, even if not instinctively, to honor the Lord's will by loving our Christian brothers and sisters (and all men) according to their present needs. This love can certainly be expressed *verbally:* there are many appropriate opportunities for sharing words of loving encouragement and admonition with one another. But the New Testament is equally clear on the point that love must be expressed *visibly:* if there is something that we can do for our brother beyond a compassionate, gentle word, we must do it. We must do it because it is right to love one's brother. Good feelings will follow good actions.

---

[116]Heb. 13:1-3, 16.

11

HOW WE SHARE

Paul's Epistle to the Romans has long been recognized by the church as prominent among all her founding documents. Written near the conclusion of his third and final missionary journey, it addresses a Christian community of Jews and Gentiles as yet unfamiliar to Paul, except by their worldwide reputation as "believers." In that renowned characteristic, the apostle found not only something for which to thank God, but also the unifying factor that could bind this culturally divided group of Christians into a true fellowship. Paul was especially concerned about the unity of the church in Rome, not only because of its strategic cultural importance at the heart of the Empire, but also because division among Christians there would represent a crucial challenge to his inspired vision of God's will in Christ Jesus: that God's people of all cultural backgrounds live together in "righteousness, peace and joy in the Holy Spirit."[117]

The Character Of Christianity In Rome

The Christians of Rome are not addressed as a single congregation. The greeting is conspicuous for its lack of Paul's usual description of God's people as the *ekklesia* (church), and yet it seems obvious that the entire Christian population of Rome is to receive the letter:

> To all in Rome who are loved by God and called to be saints....[118]

It is not simply the absence of the designation, "church," that points toward a divided Christian community at Rome, however. There were other churches to whom Paul wrote who likewise were not greeted as such; yet, we have no reason to doubt that they lived and worshipped together in unity as one body. Although these churches didn't necessarily meet together under one roof on a weekly basis, their essential unity in Christ was intact. There was no cultural gap threatening to produce two distinct Christianities, two separate churches. However, the Epistle to the Romans contains evidence of just such a cultural chasm existing among the early Roman Christians. An overview of Romans 14:1-15:7 will not only reveal the problem of division among Roman Christians of the first century, but will also help us understand the problem of disunity in our own day, as well as God's solutions for it at the local level.

---

[117]Rom. 14:17.   [118]Rom. 1:7.

The Situation: Division Over Nonessentials

The situation that Paul addresses in Romans 14 can be deduced from the opening verses of the chapter, when we supplement that information with what we learn from 1 Cor. 8-10 and extra-biblical cultural studies of the ancient world.

> *Accept him whose faith is weak, without passing judgment on disputable matters. One man's faith allows him to eat everything, but another man, whose faith is weak, eats only vegetables. The man who eats everything must not look down on him who does not, and the man who does not eat everything must not condemn the man who does, for God has accepted him. Who are you to judge someone else's servant? To his own master he stands or falls. And he will stand, for the Lord is able to make him stand. One man considers one day more sacred than another; another man considers every day alike. Each one should be fully convinced in his own mind.[119]*

The subject of Paul's discussion throughout Romans 14 concerns differences regarding "disputable matters" among those who are equally "in Christ." Some translators call these areas of disagreement "opinions" (NASB), but the context makes it clear that both translations point to the same type of issue: *matters nonessential to salvation in Christ.* Paul is not dealing here with the clear moral and doctrinal absolutes that bind us to God and one another; he is not discussing the case of those who walk according to the flesh,[120] who return to a life of worldly wickedness,[121]

---

[119]Rom. 14:1-5.
[120]See Rom. 6:15-16, 21; 8:13; Gal. 5:19-21; 6:7-8; Col. 3:5-9.
[121]See 1 Cor. 5:11-13; 6:9-10; Eph. 5:3-7; 1 Thess. 4:1-8; 2 Peter 2:9-22; Jude 1ff; 1 John 3:4-10; 5:16-17.

who reject the sevenfold unity of the Spirit,[122] who go beyond the apostolic teaching concerning the person of Christ,[123] or who abandon the gospel in favor of some other hope of salvation.[124] There is indeed a "circle of truth" in which we must stand, but the boundaries of that circle are as much wider than those of legalism as they are narrower than those of liberalism. Within the perimeter of that circle, there is a bottomless ocean of grace: grace to cover doctrinal imperfections, as well as moral ones. The beauty of grace is that *God accepts us "in Christ"* with all of our personal weaknesses, idiosyncrasies, and failings. He cleanses us and forgives us, so that...

> *...There is now no condemnation for those who are in Christ Jesus....*[125]

Kosher, Culture, And Christ

In culturally mixed congregations of the first century, both Jews and Gentiles held to certain distinctive dietary and calendar observances that created social tensions and barriers to practical fellowship. Since the establishment of the nation Israel, the Law had enjoined strict laws of kosher that made social interaction with Gentiles a practical impossibility, and even hindered Jews from freely extending and receiving hospitality among themselves. How could a Jew be sure that his food was really kosher unless it had been prepared within his own household? Or how could a con-

---

[122]See Eph. 4:5-6.

[123]See 1 John 1:1-4; 2:22-25; 4:1-6; 5:6-10, 21; 2 John 7-11; 1 Cor. 12:13.

[124]See Gal. 1:6-9; 5:4-6; 1 Cor. 15:1-4; Col. 1:21-23; 2:6-8; John 14:6; Acts 4:12; 2 Thess. 1:8-10.

[125]Rom. 8:1; compare 1 John 1:5-10.

verted Gentile buy meat at the market place, when he knew that it had probably been sacrificed to the idol from which he had turned in order to serve the living God? It took a revelation from heaven to convince the apostle Peter that Christ had set him free from cultural taboos so that he could enter the house of a Gentile and share Israel's Good News with the uncircumcised.[126] Had he not heard Christ speak clearly on this issue before?

> *Again Jesus called the crowd to him and said, "Listen to me, everyone, and understand this. Nothing outside a man can make him 'unclean' by going into him. Rather, it is what comes out of a man that makes him 'unclean'....Don't you see that nothing that enters a man from the outside can make him 'unclean'? For it doesn't go into his heart but into his stomach, and then out of his body." (In saying this, Jesus declared all foods "clean.")[127]*

But hadn't God Himself spoken through Moses in giving those laws of kosher? Who does this Jesus think He is, declaring all foods "clean"?

The Old Gives Way To The New

Jesus knew who He was: One greater than Moses, greater than Elijah and Jonah and the other prophets—even greater than the temple itself![128] With His appearing, the days of Israel's elementary education drew to a close, and the Law, in both its moral and ceremonial requirements, would find fulfillment as shadow became substance:

---

[126]See Acts 10:1-29.   [127]Mark 7:14-15, 18-19.
[128]See Matt. 5:17; 12:6, 8, 41-42; 17:1-5; compare Heb. 1:1-3.

Jesus declared, "Believe Me, woman, a time is coming when you will worship the Father neither on this mountain nor in Jerusalem." [129]

So the law was put in charge to lead us to Christ that we might be justified by faith. Now that faith has come, we are no longer under the supervision of the law. [130]

Therefore do not let anyone judge you by what you eat or drink, or with regard to a religious festival, a New Moon celebration or a Sabbath day. These are a shadow of the things that were to come; the reality, however, is found in Christ. [131]

...the way into the Most Holy Place had not yet been disclosed as long as the first tabernacle was still standing. This is an illustration for the present time, indicating that the gifts and sacrifices being offered were not able to clear the conscience of the worshiper. They are only a matter of food and drink and various ceremonial washings—external regulations applying until the time of the new order. [132]

Growing In Grace And Knowledge

Paul's understanding of Christ and the meaning of the gospel developed as the Spirit continued to guide him into deeper implications of the Christian faith. He shared his profound insights with Christians among the churches as they became mature enough to receive them. To the rest, he gave "milk"—the simpler and more basic aspects of the faith. Paul's Corinthian epistles, for example, do not

---

[129]John 4:21.   [130]Gal. 3:24-25; compare Rom. 10:4.
[131]Col. 2:16-17.   [132]Heb. 9:8-10.

present the implications of the gospel as richly as does the epistle to the Ephesians:

> *Brothers, I could not address you as spiritual but as worldly— mere infants in Christ. I gave you milk, not solid food, for you were not yet ready for it. Indeed, you are still not ready.*[133]

In his Ephesian epistle, Paul was able to share the meaning of Christ on a more profound level:

> *For he himself is our peace, who has made the two [Jew and Gentile] one and has destroyed the barrier, the dividing wall of hostility, by abolishing in his flesh the law with its commandments and regulations. His purpose was to create in himself one new man out of the two, thus making peace, and in this one body to reconcile both of them to God through the cross, by which he put to death their hostility.*[134]

From the perspective of the Law's moral requirements and ceremonial typology, Christ came to fulfill and not to abolish the Law. But Paul clearly perceived that the Law was indeed abolished (as a factor of social and spiritual hostility between Jews and other nations) when Christ fulfilled it. There were Christians from both sides of that "dividing wall," however, who were not yet ready to grasp the cultural implications of the gospel of Christ:

> *Then some of the believers who belonged to the party of the Pharisees stood up and said, "The Gentiles must be circumcised and required to obey the law of Moses."*[135]

---

[133] 1 Cor. 3:1-2.   [134] Eph. 2:14-16.
[135] Acts 15:5.

169

So then, about eating food sacrificed to idols: We know that an idol is nothing at all in the world and that there is no God but one....But not everyone knows this. Some people are still so accustomed to idols that when they eat such food they think of it as having been sacrificed to an idol, and since their conscience is weak, it is defiled.[136]

Some Jewish Christians were slow to grasp the truth of the gospel relative to freedom from the Law. Some Gentile believers were equally unprepared to fully appreciate the monotheistic implications of the gospel of Christ. Both Jewish and Gentile Christians needed to rethink certain aspects of their cultural predispositions in light of the truth of the gospel. Many Jewish Christians were "hung up" on a true, divine revelation that was no longer binding. Most Gentile believers had not enjoyed the advantage of having the divine Law to ground them in the elementary principles of true religion, and so they were "hung up" on irrelevant pagan superstitions.

Hang Ups, Issues, And Division

It is very possible that cultural or personal "hang ups" from our own backgrounds, which have no essential relationship to living in Christ, can cause divisions among Christians in local churches today. Without endorsing or denouncing either side of these issues, I will list just a few possible points of controversy and division among twentieth century brothers and sisters in Christ. No matter how strongly we may feel about these issues, remember that there are sincere Christians who hold opposite positions on these "disputable matters":

[136] 1 Cor. 8:4, 7.

1. Participation in politics, military service, and law enforcement agencies.

2. Moderate drinking of alcoholic beverages.

3. Appreciation of visual and musical art produced by non-Christians.

4. Swimming or sunbathing at public beaches.

5. Dancing.

6. Smoking.

7. Going to movies.

8. Watching television.

9. The indwelling and working of the Holy Spirit.

10. The Bible's teaching about divorce and remarriage.

11. The emphasis and procedure of church assemblies.

12. The Bible's teaching about the "last things" (the end of the present age).

13. Educating of children in the home.

14. Fashion (hair style, clothing fads, slang speech).

15. Arcade games.

16. Lotteries and other "games of chance."

Will we divide the body of Christ over these and many other such issues? Will we have a "meat eating" church and a "non-meat eating" church? How about a "health food and jogging" communion, as opposed to the "junk food" fellowship?

The Solution: Let Christ Be Lord And God Be Judge

Paul's solution to the problem of church division over nonessential matters involves a recognition of Christ's lordship and an acceptance of one another:

> *He who regards one day as special, does so to the Lord. He who eats meat, eats to the Lord, for he gives thanks to God; and he who abstains, does so to the Lord and gives thanks to God. For none of us lives to himself alone and none of us dies to himself alone. If we live, we live to the Lord; and if we die, we die to the Lord. So, whether we live or die, we belong to the Lord. For this very reason, Christ died and returned to life so that he might be the Lord of both the dead and the living. You, then, why do you judge your brother? Or why do you look down on your brother? For we will all stand before God's judgment seat....Therefore let us stop passing judgment on one another.*[137]

There is only one Lord to whom each believer is answerable, and only one God who is able to judge the motives and intentions of each heart.[138] Paul reminded Christians that, since "love believes all things," we should not impute bad motives to one another. We must *believe* in one another, realizing that each Christian is striving to please the

---

[137]Rom. 14:6-13.
[138]See 1 Chron. 28:9; Ps. 7:9; 44:20-21; Prov. 15:11; 17:3; 21:2; 24:12; Jer. 11:20; 17:10; 20:12; Acts 1:24; 8:22; 15:8; Rom. 8:27; 1 Thess. 2:4; Heb. 4:13; Rev. 2:23.

Lord, whether he "eats" or "abstains." Much harm is done by those who presume to judge the motives behind another Christian's actions. Such criticism is destructive to the body of Christ and its individual members. It also dishonors the one Lord who alone is qualified to judge all mankind, since only *He* has triumphed over sin and death by His own sinless life, atoning death, and glorious resurrection. God, in Christ, receives and accepts each person who lives by faith in Him. The solution to the problem of division over "disputable matters" is a unanimous agreement in this central, non-disputable matter: *Jesus is Lord.*

Accept one another, then, just as Christ accepted you, in order to bring praise to God.[139]

The Pharisaic Spirit

Self-righteous Pharisaism is alive and well, unfortunately. We still have those censorious, judgmental individuals among us who make a profession of finding fault with brothers and sisters whose convictions and practices in non-

---

[139]Rom. 15:7. Compare Rom. 14:1. Consider the words of the song, "We Are One" (©1988 by Keith and Sanna Luker):

If just once I could know how it feels to be a part
  Of a body that is one in heart and soul,
Then the Lord would smile on us, count us faithful to His trust
  Of the precious blood of Jesus Christ, His Son.

Fellow people of God, won't you flow together now?
  Be the church that Jesus Christ died to save!
Children of the Most High God, He has called us each to die
And become the lovely body of the Lord.

If the people who love God and claim Jesus as their Lord
(continued)

essential matters differ from their own. Each of us must guard against this Pharisaic tendency:

> *"Do not judge, or you too will be judged. For in the same way you judge others, you will be judged, and with the measure you use, it will be measured to you. Why do you look at the speck of sawdust in your brother's eye and pay no attention to the plank in your own eye? How can you say to your brother, 'Let me take the speck out of your eye,' when all the time there is a plank in your own eye? You hypocrite, first take the plank out of your own eye, and then you will see clearly to remove the speck from your brother's eye."* [140]

> *At that time Jesus went through the grainfields on the Sabbath. His disciples were hungry and began to pick some heads of grain and eat them. When the Pharisees saw this, they said to him, "Look! Your disciples are doing what is unlawful on the Sabbath."* [141]

> *Then some Pharisees and teachers of the law came to Jesus from Jerusalem and asked, "Why do your disciples break the tradition of the elders? They don't wash their hands before they eat!"* [142]

May God deliver us from this ugly spirit of gnat-straining Pharisaism! We will accept one another in the Lord only when and if we first accept the Lord Himself. The Phari-

---

Would deny their silly doctrines that divide,
If we all would recognize that the business of our Lord
Is much more than playing church on Sunday morn!

We are one! We are one!
Don't you see the walls we've made are in our minds?
We are one in the Son; let the children that are free
Remind both you and me that we are one!

[140]Matt. 7:1-5.   [141]Matt. 12:1-2.   [142]Matt. 15:1-2.

sees' condemnation of the Lord's disciples was rooted in their disrespect for Jesus. If we live to honor Christ, we will go out of our way to avoid harming His workmanship: our brothers and sisters for whom Christ died.

> *Instead, make up your mind not to put any stumbling block or obstacle in your brother's way. As one who is in the Lord Jesus, I am fully convinced that no food is unclean in itself. But if anyone regards something as unclean, then for him it is unclean. If your brother is distressed because of what you eat, you are no longer acting in love. Do not by your eating destroy your brother for whom Christ died....For the kingdom of God is not a matter of eating and drinking, but of righteousness, peace and joy in the Holy Spirit....Let us therefore make every effort to do what leads to peace and to mutual edification.*[143]

> *But food does not bring us near to God; we are no worse if we do not eat, and no better if we do. Be careful, however, that the exercise of your freedom does not become a stumbling block to the weak. For if anyone with a weak conscience sees you who have this knowledge eating in an idol's temple, won't he be emboldened to eat what has been sacrificed to idols? So this weak brother, for whom Christ died, is destroyed by your knowledge. When you sin against your brothers in this way and wound their weak conscience, you sin against Christ. Therefore, if what I eat causes my brother to fall into sin, I will never eat meat again, so that I will not cause him to fall.*[144]

Maturity And Responsibility In Christ

Growing up together in God's family means that we will learn to live responsibly with one another, practicing sin-

---

[143]Rom. 14:13-15, 17, 19.   [144]1 Cor. 8:8-13.

cere love toward one another. We are our brother's keepers in Christ. We must get our priorities straight: the spiritual health of our brothers and sisters, for whom Christ died, is infinitely more important than our personal freedoms and proper understandings in nonessential matters. A member of the body can grow only if it remains united to the head. If it is "cut off" for being less than perfect, it will die before it even approaches its potential maturity. If a member will not respond to its head, it is no longer truly a member and usually must be amputated, lest the gangrene of spiritual rebellion threaten the life of the rest of the body. But far too often, members of the body of Christ have been cut off from the life of the body *because some opinionated members assumed the place of the Head and equated their own strong convictions about nonessential issues with the Lord's requirements.* Some people will doubtless welcome Paul's teaching about liberty and mutual acceptance in Christ as an opportunity to "continue in sin that grace may abound." Paul wasn't endorsing libertinism, but he certainly wasn't recommending legalism: the binding of laws where God has bound none. Paul was talking about the way of *love*, which seeks to glorify God by living in a way that draws people to Christ while avoiding unnecessary offense toward anyone:

> *So whether you eat or drink or whatever you do, do it all for the glory of God. Do not cause anyone to stumble, whether Jews, Greeks or the church of God—even as I try to please everybody in every way. For I am not seeking my own good, but the good of many, so that they may be saved. Follow my example, as I follow the example of Christ.*[145]

---

[145] 1 Cor. 10:31-11:1.

Weaker Brothers Or False Brothers?

It is the nature of love, as demonstrated in the life and death
of Jesus, to seek the ultimate good of others (that is, their
eternal salvation), rather than one's own will. Paul would
rather forego any exercise of liberty than cause spiritual
harm to any person, whether Jew, Greek, or Christian (one
whose heritage and citizenship transcend earthly categories). But neither Jesus nor Paul would yield to the demands
of those who would negate the truth of the gospel by adding
requirements for salvation that God had not authorized.
Such people were not "weaker brothers," but *false* brothers.
Far from stumbling over the temptation to imitate a stronger brother's faith and thus sin against their own con-
sciences, these legalists were *themselves* stumbling blocks
who threatened to uproot the faith of those in whom Christ
was not yet fully formed. They would answer to God for
their perversion of the gospel and their destruction of God's
work:

> *Evidently some people are throwing you into confusion and
> are trying to pervert the gospel of Christ....If anybody is
> preaching to you a gospel other than what you accepted, let
> him be eternally condemned!*[146]

> *This matter arose because some false brothers had infiltrated
> our ranks to spy on the freedom we have in Christ Jesus and
> to make us slaves. We did not give in to them for a moment, so
> that the truth of the gospel might remain with you.*[147]

---

[146]Gal. 1:7-9.   [147]Gal. 2:4-5.

177

I am confident in the Lord that you will take no other view. The one who is throwing you into confusion will pay the penalty, whoever he may be.[148]

A "stumbling block" or "obstacle" (Paul practically equates the two terms in Rom. 14:13) is not merely "something about us that somebody else doesn't like"; it is something about us that is destructive to the spiritual life of another:

From that time on Jesus began to explain to his disciples that he must go to Jerusalem and suffer many things....Peter took him aside and began to rebuke him. "Never, Lord!" he said. "This shall never happen to you!" Jesus turned and said to Peter, "Out of my sight, Satan! You are a stumbling block to me; you do not have in mind the things of God, but the things of men."[149]

God's Interests, Or Man's?

Disciples can become stumbling blocks when they forget God's interests and replace a divine perspective with a human one. This is exactly what Jesus steadfastly refused to do, even when faced with a humiliating and excruciating death. His approach to both living and dying was, "Not My will, but Thine." Paul also lived by an inflexible commitment to the will of God which, paradoxically, required him to be extremely adaptable to the cultural biases of men:

To the Jews I became like a Jew, to win the Jews. To those under the law I became like one under the law (though I

---

[148]Gal. 5:10.

[149]Matt. 16:21-23. A "stumbling block" can also be something in another person or in oneself that results in one's own spiritual undoing. See Rom. 9:30-33; 1 Peter 2:4-8; Matt. 18:6-9.

178

myself am not under the law), so as to win those under the law. To those not having the law I became like one not having the law (though I am not free from God's law but am under Christ's law), so as to win those not having the law....I have become all things to all men so that by all possible means I might save some.[150]

How could Paul so flatly denounce those who wanted to bind circumcision and the law on the Galatian churches, when he himself had Timothy circumcised, and would later subject himself to Jewish ceremonial law at the temple in Jerusalem?[151] It is because he was "under Christ's law," the law of selfless love which places God's desire for the salvation of all men above one's personal rights, liberties, and opinions. Paul would not budge on the issue of salvation through faith in Jesus Christ, for he agreed with Peter:

"Salvation is found in no one else, for there is no other name under heaven given to men by which we must be saved." [152]

But salvation by faith in Christ (God's will for all men) was so important to Paul that *anything* which was not essentially related to that issue was set aside as unimportant by comparison. With this observation, we return to Paul's solution to the threat of division among the Roman Christians:

Do not destroy the work of God for the sake of food. All food is clean, but it is wrong for a man to eat anything that causes someone else to stumble. It is better not to eat meat or drink wine or to do anything else that will cause your brother to fall.[153]

---

[150]1 Cor. 9:20-22.
[151]See Gal. 5:2-4. Compare Acts 16:1-3; 21:20-27.
[152]Acts 4:12.   [153]Rom. 14:20-21.

Paul refused to take sides in controversies over nonessential matters, although he clearly believed that the weaker Christians' criticisms of their meat-eating brothers were unfounded. Nevertheless, the apostle did not urge the stronger brothers to convert the weaker to a "meat-eating" expression of faith. An unrestricted command to "eat" or "not eat" would have been a victory for legalism and a loss of liberty in Christ. Since only the stronger brother could either "eat" or "not eat" with a clear conscience toward God, it was his responsibility to exercise liberty in a responsible, loving, Christlike way. The weaker brother was bound by the convictions of his own conscience, and therefore could not eat without expressing a lawless, faithless attitude toward God.

Situation Ethics Versus Christian Ethics

All Christians are "weak" in some nonessential areas and "strong" in others, but whatever we do, or refrain from doing, must proceed from a sincere, personal conviction that "Jesus Christ is Lord":

> So whatever you believe about these things keep between yourself and God. Blessed is the man who does not condemn himself by what he approves. But the man who doubts is condemned if he eats, because his eating is not from faith; and everything that does not come from faith is sin.[154]

Although one Christian's expression of faith in Christ may differ from another's, this does not rule out moral absolutes, as in modern situation ethics. The law of Christ governs the Christian, and His law is love. Love is defined in terms of what Christ has done for His people and for all

---

[154]Rom. 14:22-23.

mankind:

> "My command is this: Love each other as I have loved you. Greater love has no one than this, that one lay down his life for his friends." [155]

> We who are strong ought to bear with the failings of the weak and not to please ourselves. Each of us should please his neighbor for his good, to build him up. For even Christ did not please himself. [156]

The *situation* is not lord—*Christ* is. We honor Christ as Lord when we refrain from judging our stronger brothers by laws that Christ has not bound. The Lord is glorified when we identify with the weaknesses of the weak instead of insisting on our own rights and liberties. Jesus "did not consider equality with God something to be grasped," [157] but surrendered Himself so that we might be saved. He calls each of us to let go of our personal rights, liberties, and judgements so that the body of Christ might not be divided, nor even a single member destroyed.

In Summary

How, then, can many different members share life and mature together in one body? How can they maintain a unity and love for each other strong enough to withstand the tensions of their cultural differences and individual idiosyncrasies? We must heed Paul's admonition to the body of Christ at Rome. Although the cultural distinctions between Jews and Gentiles had once been crucial, Paul considered such matters to be nonessential in Christ. [158] In Christ, all

---

[155]John 15:12-13.   [156]Rom. 15:1-3.
[157]Phil. 2:6.   [158]See Gal.5:6; 6:15. Compare Rom.4:1ff.

men and women are children of Abraham; all answer to the same God; all are justified by the same faith; all serve the same risen Lord:

> *I am not ashamed of the gospel, because it is the power of God for the salvation of everyone who believes: first for the Jew, then for the Gentile.*[159]

> *Is God the God of Jews only? Is he not the God of Gentiles too? Yes, of Gentiles too, since there is only one God, who will justify the circumcised by faith and the uncircumcised through that same faith.*[160]

> *For there is no difference between Jew and Gentile—the same Lord is Lord of all and richly blesses all who call on him....*[161]

Let Jesus Christ be the "one Lord" and let the "one God" be judge. This is God's solution to the problems of mutual acceptance and unity among members of the one body of Christ. The life that we share as members one of another is of far greater importance than what we believe about food, drink, holiday observances, and such "disputable matters":

> *For the kingdom of God is not a matter of eating and drinking, but of righteousness, peace and joy in the Holy Spirit....*[162]

---

[159]Rom. 1:16. [160]Rom. 3:29-30.
[161]Rom. 10:12. [162]Rom. 14:17.

SCRIPTURE INDEX

(Bold type shows direct quotations.)

184

185

"The blessed, will eat
the fruit of their labor"

Part Three

The Labor Of Christ

Through Us:

Every Member

A

Minister

"If you and I
were as committed,
in attitude and action,
to the body of Christ as is Jesus,
the Head,
what would be seen?"

Introductory Reflections:
Part Three

This is the the third and final volume of a series of studies that I have been teaching in Bible classes and seminars for a number of years. The response to these classes has been the primary motivation for putting the material into print.

The principles presented in *The Love Of Christ In The Local Congregation, The Life Of Christ We Share: Members One Of Another,* and now, *The Labor Of Christ Through Us: Every Member A Minister* are wonderful concepts in God's Word. These truths that spring from the gospel—the cross of Christ—should be the heartbeat and lifeblood of the people of God.

However, I'm quite certain that, in the main, these marvelous truths are not emphasized in most churches. I am also convinced that when the Lord's people take these biblical principals to heart and make continuous application of them in a genuine spiritual attitude, we will be what He desires us to be: a people loving Jesus and one another without hypocrisy, truly devoted to each other's well-being. And each one of us will be ministering, to the building up of the body of Christ according to our individual gifts and abilities.

Then, the world will see a difference in the church, for there will be a world of difference to see!

Larry Deason

12

THE BIBLICAL CONCEPT OF CHRISTIAN COMMUNITY

Myths And Misconceptions Versus Mutual Ministry

When you hear the word "church," what pictures immediately develop in your mind? Psychologists have devised a technique called "word association" in order to unmask certain misconceptions that hinder personal growth and healthy relationships among human beings. Christians do well to question secular psychology's definitions of "growth," "health," and "maturity." However, by using the word association method, we may find some of our own concepts in need of redefinition.

To most people, the linguistic symbol "c-h-u-r-c-h" primarily brings to mind the image of a huge medieval structure, complete with steeple, high ceilings, great pillars, stained glass windows, relics, and uncomfortable furniture. These people are like the little elderly lady filling out an admissions form at the hospital. She answered the question, "What is your church preference?" by writing, "Red brick"!

192

Some people get beyond the physical cathedral concept, to vague impressions of the uses that people might make of such an edifice: the holding of business meetings and solemn assemblies, the conducting of weddings and funerals. A very few people will penetrate their initial impression even more deeply. The thought that usually pops up in their minds in response to "church" will be "institution" (or some other impersonal, clinical, sterile concept like "organization" or "denomination").

Consider this scenario: large, sterile rooms full of somber, unsmiling faces; irrelevant sermons and big "god words" that make us feel small; songs that defy all attempts at enjoyment. If we seek deliverance from our ecclesiastical nightmare in the real world of English grammars and dictionaries, we are only plunged deeper beneath its distorted spell. Indeed, many theological myths and misconceptions are perpetuated by those who try to define biblical terms by consulting an English dictionary instead of a Bible lexicon:

> *church:*
> 1. a building for public and esp.
>   Christian worship
> 2. the clergy or officialdom of some
>   religious body....[1]

Webster's primary definitions of "church" reinforce popular misconceptions that hide the glory of the church and inhibit its growth. Weak ideas can never produce powerful realities; right thinking and righteous living cannot be derived from warped concepts. The common notion that God's eter-

---

[1] *Webster's Ninth New Collegiate Dictionary* (Springfield: Merriam-Webster, Inc., 1983), p. 240.

nally purposed church, for which Christ endured the horrors of the cross, is merely a building-bound institution or religious hierarchy, represents one of the Deceiver's most effective distortions of the truth.

> *[God's] intent was that now, through the church, the manifold wisdom of God should be made known to the rulers and authorities in the heavenly realms, according to his eternal purpose which he accomplished in Christ Jesus our Lord....Now to him who is able to do immeasurably more than all we ask or imagine, according to his power that is at work within us, to him be glory in the church and in Christ Jesus throughout all generations, forever and ever! Amen.*[2]

> *Now I rejoice in what was suffered for you, and I fill up in my flesh what is still lacking in regard to Christ's afflictions, for the sake of his body, which is the church.*[3]

Organism, Not Organization

The Spirit of God who speaks through the biblical writers describes the church as "the body of Christ." Here is the difference between what is commonly thought of as "the church" and what is biblically presented as "the church": *the church is not an organization, but a living organism.* An organized pattern of cells may or may not be more than a mere "organization." The characteristic that distinguishes the organism from mere organization is *life* within the organism.

Contrary to popular evolutionary thinking, greater complexity within an organism does not always improve the quality of its life. God indeed has equipped the various cre-

---

[2]Eph. 3:10-11, 20-21.   [3]Col. 1:24.

ated "kinds" of organisms with the capacity to respond and adapt to environmental changes and conditions, in order to preserve and promote the well-being of each "kind." But a fish would not improve the quality of its fish-life by exchanging its "primitive" fins for a "complex" set of arms and legs! Its attempts to survive in the water would be as short-lived as its attempts to live on the land.

Institutionalization And Fossilization

Congregations (and church members) who forget that organization is subservient to *life* fall into the trap of *institutionalization*. They mistakenly believe that the health and growth of the church ultimately depend on human ingenuity in finding and preserving the right forms, structures, and programs. In time, they forget the principle that forms and organization exist to serve human life in Christ, and not vice versa:

> One Sabbath Jesus was going through the grainfields, and as his disciples walked along, they began to pick some heads of grain. The Pharisees said to him, "Look, why are they doing what is unlawful on the Sabbath?" He answered, "Have you never read what David did when he and his companions were hungry and in need? In the days of Abiathar the high priest, he entered the house of God and ate the consecrated bread, which is lawful only for priests to eat. And he also gave some to his companions." Then he said to them, "**The Sabbath was made for man, not man for the Sabbath.** So the Son of Man is Lord even of the Sabbath."[4]

> Since you are eager to have spiritual gifts, try to excel in gifts that **build up the church**....What then shall we say, brothers?

---

[4]Mark 2:23-28. Compare Matt. 12:1-8; Luke 6:1-5.

195

> *When you come together, everyone has a hymn, or a word of instruction, a revelation, a tongue or an interpretation. All of these must be done for the **strengthening of the church**....For you can all prophesy in turn so that everyone may be **instructed and encouraged**....For God is not a God of disorder but of peace.*[5]

What you or I believe about the Sabbath or miraculous spiritual gifts may be either nearer to or farther from the truth. Like many doctrinal issues that divide the body of Christ, these matters are beside the present point. My point is that institutionalism ultimately will choke the life out of any church. The remedy is to maintain proper priorities. Forms and order are important, but only as they serve the goal of promoting life among God's people, to the praise of His glory.

A church which seeks final answers and security in organizational forms will find itself forgetting what it was called to be in the world: the *living body* of Christ. Institutionalism is too worldly to be healthy for the body of Christ, and too "churchy" to be relevant to the needs of the unredeemed world. It makes the church a "fish out of water," and a fish out of water does not adapt to its "other world" environment, it succumbs to it—by slowly languishing, and finally, dying.

Errors usually come in pairs. From the extreme of seeking security in institutional forms, we may go to the opposite extreme of forgetting that a living organism must adapt to changes in its *own* environment to survive and thrive. Just because forms and programs are not the essence of the church's life does not mean that they have no place at all.

------

[5]1 Cor. 14:12, 26, 31, 33.

196

Christians *will* interact and influence one another, and this means that some type of format or structure is inevitable. The only question is whether those forms will be orderly or chaotic, edifying or discouraging, helpful or harmful, invigorating or numbing. We can have effective forms or ineffective forms, but we *will have forms* of some sort.

In the following directives I have no praise for you, for your meetings do more harm than good.[6]

Churches that refuse to be responsive to the needs of the members of the body of Christ and of the "watching world" in choosing and (when necessary) changing forms become *fossilized.* Members of the body of Christ need forms that will enable them to exercise their abilities in ministering to one another.

The unredeemed world needs to see that the Spirit of Christ is active in and through the members of the body of Christ. Too often, churches are stifled and stunted by the "we've always done it this way" mentality. *Living organisms* have the capacity to grow, adapt, and respond to the immediate environment. Institutionalism and fossilization hinder the health of the body of Christ, and, if unchecked, can even choke the life out of a Christian community.

Not Institutional, But "Organismal"

Whether the figure is that of a body, a bride, or a building, the Bible consistently speaks of the people of God as being *alive* in their relationship to God and to one another.

---

[6]1 Cor. 11:17.

197

Instead, speaking the truth in love, we will in all things grow up into him who is the Head, that is, Christ. From him the whole body, joined and held together by every supporting ligament, grows and builds itself up in love, as each part does its work.[7]

For the husband is the head of the wife as Christ is the head of the church, his body, of which he is the Savior.[8]

As you come to him, the living Stone—rejected by men but chosen by God and precious to him—you also, like living stones, are being built into a spiritual house to be a holy priesthood, offering spiritual sacrifices acceptable to God through Jesus Christ.[9]

Each member of Christ's body is made alive by the blood of Christ: by participating, through faith, in the love of God which is held out to us in the gospel of Christ. The lifeblood of the body of Christ is this divine love:

But because of his great love for us, God, who is rich in mercy, made us alive with Christ even when we were dead in transgressions—it is by grace you have been saved. And God raised us up with Christ and seated us with him in the heavenly realms in Christ...[10]

Institutionalism—inordinate concern for programs and forms as the main business of the church—takes our eyes off God's power and love, by which He has called us to Himself and to one another. *It is possible* to become distracted from a pure devotion to Christ and dedication to His gospel.

---

[7]Eph.4:15-16. Compare Col.2:19.   [8]Eph. 5:23.
[9]1 Peter 2:4-5. Compare Rom. 12:1-2f.
[10]Eph. 2:4-6. Compare Rom. 1:16-17; 3:21-26; 5:6-8; 6:1ff.

An institutional emphasis can cause those who begin in the Spirit to attempt to gain perfection by the flesh (legalism); it can degenerate into an idolatrous fascination with *human religion* that has no vital connection with Christ, the Head, and *His righteousness.*[11] *True religion* is serving God by following Christ in caring for people—all people. Institutionalism tends to elevate human concerns above divine, ecclesiastical machinery above genuine discipleship, and programs above people.

But there is an alternative to institutionalism. We *can* have order and edifying forms and (yes) even people-oriented programs, without those forms and programs swallowing us up. We can determine in our hearts before God to maintain proper priorities: *life* above organization, *people* above programs, *the Lord Jesus Christ* above all our human dreams and schemes. To keep such a commitment will require constant vigilance. Institutionalistic thinking grows as luxuriantly in a "natural" mind as crabgrass on an unkept lawn. We must speak and write in such a manner as to constantly call one another back to the mind of God concerning the church, and everything else. The body must not become so preoccupied with itself that it forgets its attachment to the Head.

I have coined a word that, for me, suggests the God-ordained manner of life appropriate to the church as a living organism: *organismal.* As "organic" speaks of the nature and composition of a living thing, "organismal" conveys the style in which an organism functions and expresses its life. The body of Christ is an organism, and the members

---

[11]Note Gal. 3:1-5; Col. 2:6-3:4.

share together in the life of it's head, Christ. All the church's structure, forms, programs, and other expressions of body life must be *organismal:* they must express the nature of the Christian community as a living organism.

We do not nail a two-by-four piece of cut lumber to a living tree with the expectation that the dead wood will grow with the living tree. A living branch grafted onto a living trunk can be expected to grow, because it can assimilate and share the life of the whole tree. There is a correspondence between tree and branch that does not exist between tree and board: a correspondence of life to life and living to living. That which is dead cannot express the qualities of that which is alive, and no method of artificial attachment can overcome this deficiency! (Even in the case of organ transplants, the donated organ must be carefully preserved to retain its living properties; artificial organs cannot really share the life of the human body.)

Many forms, methods, programs, and expressions of "church life" and "church work" are similarly incompatible with the nature of the body of Christ. Dead works cannot be artificially attached to the living body of Christ, and thereby become alive. Forms, programs, methods, and structures by which the church expresses its life must flow from the power and love of the Living God. They must be expressions that are compatible with the Living Word: the Good News of God's love revealed in the Living Lord. The methods we use must be motivated by Christ's holy and compassionate Spirit at work within and among us.[12]

---

[12]See John 15:1-8; Gal. 5:22-23; Eph. 1:18-21; 3:14-21; Phil. 1:6; 2:13; Col. 1:3-6, 10-12, 25-27.

Works and forms motivated by *legalism* ("One mistake could be fatal"), blind service to *tradition* ("We've always done it this way"), *utilitarianism* ("It gets results"), or *any other basis* than the love of God in Christ Jesus are *lifeless:* dead works. Organismal forms and expressions are movements of the body of Christ which manifest the life of Christ in the world by ministering to human needs. Institutional ideas about "church life" and "church work" cannot meet the need and fulfill God's purpose, nor can they glorify Him.

> *"No one sews a patch of unshrunk cloth on an old garment. If he does, the new piece will tear away from the old, making the tear worse. And no one pours new wine into old wineskins. If he does, the wine will burst the skins, and both the wine and the wineskins will be ruined. No, he pours new wine into new wineskins."* [13]

> *All the believers were one in heart and mind. No one claimed that any of his possessions was his own, but they shared everything they had. With great power the apostles continued to testify to the resurrection of the Lord Jesus, and much grace was upon them all. There were no needy persons among them. For from time to time those who owned lands or houses sold them, brought the money from the sales and put it at the apostles' feet, and it was distributed to anyone as he had need.* [14]

Necessary Conditions For Mutual Ministry

In order to implement the organismal life-style among members of a local church or Christian community, at least four practical conditions must be present. I will present them in logical sequence with a brief discussion of each condition.

---

[13] Mark 2:21-22. Compare Matt. 9:16-17.
[14] Acts 4:32-35. Compare Acts 2:42-47.

First of all, there must be *covenant*. It may be written out or verbally expressed. It may be stated formally or informally, but it *must* express a firm commitment and mutual understanding among the body members. Covenants define the nature and conditions of a relationship, as in a marriage or a business contract. Covenants spell out each party's privileges and responsibilities in maintaining right relationships within the covenant community. In initiating covenant relationship with His people, God has always carefully and clearly unfolded the terms of His gracious offer:

> *Then Moses went up to God, and the LORD called to him from the mountain and said, "This is what you are to say to the house of Jacob and what you are to tell the people of Israel: 'You yourselves have seen what I did to Egypt, and how I carried you on eagles' wings and brought you to myself. Now if you obey me fully and keep my covenant, then out of all nations you will be my treasured possession. Although the whole earth is mine, you will be for me a kingdom of priests and a holy nation.' These are the words you are to speak to the Israelites." So Moses went back and summoned the elders of the people and set before them all the words the Lord had commanded him to speak. The people all responded together, "We will do everything the LORD has said." So Moses brought their answer back to the LORD.*[15]

In the context of Christian relationships, a covenant should involve *mutual* commitment of members, *belonging to one another* under the lordship of Christ. The covenant should provide for sharing together in worshipping the one God re-

---

[15]Exod. 19:3-9. Compare Exod. 20:1-24:18; Matt. 5:1-7:28; 28:16-20.

vealed in Scripture as Father, Son, and Spirit. There should also be fellowship in the work of the kingdom of God: proclamation of the gospel to the lost (evangelism); building up the members in knowledge of the Word (edification); caring for human needs of all kinds, certainly within the community of believers, but also beyond (benevolence). Mutual understanding of relationship and agreement to lovingly belong to one another is essential to the organismal life-style.

Community

Second, there must be *community*. Covenant lays the foundation for the reality of community. As an appendix to this book, I have listed many of the New Testament references that enjoin specific "one another" responsibilities on every Christian. These cannot be carried out with any degree of consistency apart from mutual covenant agreement to live together as a community.

Many assume that "community living" is equal to "communal life-style" (or even "communism"). But the New Testament demands concerning Christian discipleship and individual stewardship do not necessarily involve the abolition of personal property. Even in New Testament descriptions of communal life-style among early Christians (for example, in Acts 2:42-47 and 4:32-35), all sharing was to be done on a volunteer basis, motivated by immediate needs and spontaneous love.[16]

---

[16]See Acts 5:1-4; 2 Cor. 8:7-9; 9:6-7; Phil. 4:10-19; Gal. 2:10; Acts 11:27-30.

Community members are free, in Christ, to live in separate dwellings or under one roof. We can choose to pool our resources into a common treasury or retain personal oversight of the assets with which the Lord blesses us. What we are *not* free to do is to close our hearts and our homes toward God's needy children, our brothers and sisters for whom Jesus Christ gave His life:

> *"Then the King will say to those on his right, 'Come, you who are blessed by my Father; take your inheritance, the kingdom prepared for you since the creation of the world. For I was hungry and you gave me something to eat, I was thirsty, and you gave me something to drink, I was a stranger and you invited me in, I needed clothes and you clothed me, I was sick and you looked after me, I was in prison and you came to visit me....I tell you the truth, whatever you did for the least of these brothers of mine, you did for me....whatever you did not do for one of the least of these, you did not do for me.'"* [17]

> *Keep on loving each other as brothers. Do not forget to entertain strangers, for by so doing some people have entertained angels without knowing it. Remember those in prison as if you were their fellow prisoners, and those who are mistreated as if you yourselves were suffering.* [18]

> *Offer hospitality to one another without grumbling. Each one should use whatever gift he has received to serve others, faithfully administering God's grace in its various forms.* [19]

> *If anyone has material possessions and sees his brother in need but has no pity on him, how can the love of God be in him?* [20]

---

[17] Matt. 25:34-36, 40,45. See also Matt. 5:42.
[18] Heb. 13:1-3. See also Rom. 12:13.
[19] 1 Peter 4:9-11. See also Gal. 6:6-10; 3 John 5-8.
[20] 1 John 3:17. See also James 2:14-17.

Loving and sharing, as good stewards of God's trust, are not optional in Christ; these are the *essence* of living "in Christ." There may be different ways of expressing Christian community among groups of believers, but *community must be expressed.* There must be the reality of self-sacrifice for the sake of others. Isolationism and individualism are no part of the Christian life-style described in the Bible. We are called to set aside our selfishness by contributing our unique individuality to the building up of the body of Christ. In losing our individualism (self-centeredness), we find our individuality (true identity as unique members of the body of Christ). Broken homes and divided churches are caused by those who have been deceived into believing that they can be true to themselves by being false to their commitments and responsibilities.

Communion

The third condition necessary for the realization of the organismal way of life among God's people is *communion:* participation together in a common life or venture.[21] Often, this sharing of a common life was expressed in table fellowship: the common meal. Conversely, a refusal to eat with someone was a statement of alienation and disassociation from that person:

> *Every day they continued to meet together in the temple courts. They broke bread in their homes and ate together with glad and sincere hearts....*[22]

[21]From the Greek *koinonia,* also translated "sharing" and "fellowship," or "partnership."
[22]Acts 2:46. Compare 1 Cor. 5:11.

When Peter came to Antioch, I opposed him to his face, because he was in the wrong. Before certain men came from James, he used to eat with the Gentiles. But when they arrived, he began to draw back and separate himself because he was afraid of those who belonged to the circumcision group.[23]

"Here I am! I stand at the door and knock. If anyone hears my voice and opens the door, I will come in and eat with him, and he with me."[24]

Nothing touched by the Spirit of Christ remains common (ordinary, "secular"); the "common meal" became the *agape* (love) feast, a meal shared among early Christians to express their oneness in sharing life in Christ. This meal, in turn, became the setting in which the covenant meal instituted by the Lord Jesus was shared among His disciples:

They devoted themselves to the apostles' teaching and to the fellowship, to the breaking of bread and to prayer.[25]

*Is not the cup of thanksgiving for which we give thanks a participation [**koinonia**: communion] in the blood of Christ? And is not the bread that we break a participation [koinonia] in the body of Christ? Because there is one loaf, we, who are many, are one body, for we all partake of the one loaf.*[26]

---

[23]Gal. 2:11-12. Compare Acts 11:2-3.
[24]Rev. 3:20.   [25]Acts 2:42. Compare Acts 20:7.
[26]1 Cor. 10:16-17. Compare 1 Cor. 11:17-34, where Paul denounces the Corinthian church's abuse of the Lord's Supper in its *agape* feast context. The sharing of the bread and cup were intended to be a sign of covenant unity among the members. The shameful gluttony and selfish conduct of the Corinthian Christians at their "love feast" was a negation of the example and presence of the Lord of the covenant; they could not express their sharing of life in Christ while they ignored and despised one another. The meaning of the Lord's Supper as a "communion" with Christ and one another was being spoiled by their unloving, inconsiderate behavior at the "love feast."

The communion meal (Lord's Supper) is simultaneously a dramatization of the gospel that binds the Christian community to the Lord and to one another, and an expression of the unity of that community. The reality of communion (shared life in Christ) is not limited to any single expression of it, whether the Lord's Supper, a pot-luck dinner, or whatever.

The life shared by members of the Christian community is based on the redemptive work of Christ, a fact which is celebrated and reaffirmed with every sharing of the Lord's Supper. The sharing of life *with* Christ and *in* Christ that centers around the Lord's Supper should flow out from that center to touch every aspect of our lives, as a stone which is thrown into a still pond will send ripples from its center to its outermost edges. Christ is the Stone that disturbs the stagnant pond of our self-centeredness. His impact on our lives should cause waves of ever-widening involvement in caring for one another.

Commitment

The fourth element in organismal life among God's people is *commitment*. The three previously mentioned factors (covenant, community, and communion) are all dependent on this one. Each of us must hold a deep and firm personal commitment to the Lord Jesus Christ and His body, the church; to love Jesus is to love what He loves.

To be committed to Jesus is to be committed to what He is committed to. Since Jesus emptied Himself of heavenly glory and gave His life for His church, and for each individual member of it, it is axiomatic that Christians must accept, love, and serve one another. We are brought together in one body on the basis of Christ's death and resurrection. And on that basis, we *must* accept one another, in all of our wonderful diversities and our not-so-wonderful idiosyncracies. If we can view one another as blood-bought parts of a living body rather than as manufactured, interchangeable cogs in an institutional machine, then *diversity* among the members of the Christian community can be seen in a positive light, and not as a threat or something negative.

Do nothing out of selfish ambition or vain conceit, but in humility consider others better than yourselves. Each of you should look not only to your own interests, but also to the interests of others. Your attitude should be the same as that of Christ Jesus....[27]

I am jealous for you with a godly jealousy. I promised you to one husband, to Christ, so that I might present you as a pure virgin to him....Besides everything else, I face daily the pressure of my concern for all the churches. Who is weak, and I do not feel weak? Who is led into sin, and I do not inwardly burn?[28]

For by the grace given me I say to every one of you: Do not think of yourself more highly than you ought....Just as each of us has one body with many members, and these members do not all have the same function, so in Christ we who are many form one body, and each member belongs to all the others.[29]

The eye cannot say to the hand, "I don't need you!" And the head cannot say to the feet, "I don't need you!" ...But God has combined the members of the body and has given greater honor to the parts that lacked it, so that there should be no division in the body, but that its parts should have equal concern for each other. If one part suffers, every part suffers with

---

[27]Phil. 2:3-5.   [28]2 Cor. 11:2, 28-29.   [29]Rom. 12:3-5.

it; if one part is honored, every part rejoices with it. Now you are the body of Christ, and each one of you is a part of it.[30]

We who are strong ought to bear with the failings of the weak and not to please ourselves. Each of us should please his neighbor for his good, to build him up. For even Christ did not please himself....Accept one another, then, just as Christ accepted you, in order to bring praise to God.[31]

Community Is An Attitude: "Come, Unity!"

Behind these practical conditions, which are essential for implementing the biblical (organismal) life-style among a group of believers, there must be the deliberate adoption of proper attitudes. Community spirit transforms a group of disciples into a vital organism. Without this attitude, none of the conditions of true Christian togetherness can be realized. Let us finally realize that community-togetherness (like all other virtues) and sectarian-apartness (like all other sins) are not external entities. There is no pot of gold "out there" to seek, any more than there is a boogey man "out there" to fear.

Sectarianism and community spirit are both "heart conditions";[32] they are attitudes of the inner man, planted within us either by the spirit who dominates the unregenerate world (Satan), or the Spirit of God, respectively. Our emphasis in reforming, restoring, and reviving the people of

---

[30]1 Cor. 12:21, 24-27.   [31]Rom. 15:1-3, 7.

[32]Note Matthew 15:19-20 (compare Mark 7:20-23); Gal. 5:19-23; James 1:13-15. Jesus repeatedly warned against making external concerns the primary emphasis in spiritual matters: "The kingdom of God does not come visibly, nor will people say, 'Here it is,' or 'There it is,' because the kingdom of God is within you" (Luke 17:20; see also Matt. 23:23-28; 5:17-6:18).

209

God should not center on outward forms and structures, but on inward beliefs and attitudes. Human conduct flows outward from the convictions and attitudes that are held within. That is why Jesus' approach to righteousness ("from the inside, out") clashes so fundamentally with the sectarian's approach ("on the outside only"). Symptoms of spiritual sickness may be temporarily covered up by application of external measures, but inward maladies cannot be *cured* except by inward treatment. That is why the focus of this book is not on gimmicks, techniques, and programs which purport to manufacture from the outside what the Spirit of God must create from the inside! Rather, we will concern ourselves with right understandings of biblical principles and attitudes, and the practical application of these principles and attitudes.

A Word To Leaders

One of the most wonderful biblical principles with which we must reckon is expressed beautifully by Deborah, a woman raised up by God to lead a work of deliverance for which no man in Israel would accept responsibility:

> *"When the princes in Israel take the lead, when the people willingly offer themselves—praise the Lord!"*[33]

Throughout history, the point is illustrated again and again, both positively and negatively: those in positions of leadership among God's people set the example and the tone for the life of the people. Preachers, elders, deacons, and teachers can recognize and respond to the biblical teaching con-

---

[33]Judges 5:2.

cerning Christian community by taking their proper place *as servants* among the other members of the body; or, they can seek to carve out for themselves a secure place at the top of a tottering power structure by refusing to let Jesus Christ be the only Head of His body. Such a refusal is, of course, futile and fatal to the desired end. No structure that sets itself against the lordship of Christ can ultimately stand; no life that seeks its own security instead of the kingdom of God will be saved. By casting out the Heir of the LORD's vineyard, the Jewish leaders only succeeded in assuring Christ's triumph and their own downfall at the hands of the Roman general Titus.

Christ is Head of His body; *every member* of His body is placed there by God Himself to minister to his or her fellow-members, to the glory of God. The authority of leaders among God's people is a delegated authority, not absolute power. It is authority to feed sheep, tend lambs, and protect the flock from savage wolves; in short, it is the power to serve. Anyone who assumes authority beyond what Christ has delegated for the building up of His people is a thief and a robber, setting himself up as a rival of Christ. Even true apostles were simply servant-members of the body, and would not presume the authority of the Head. To serve a "rival Christ" is to worship an idol:

> *As Peter entered the house, Cornelius met him and fell at his feet in reverence. But Peter made him get up. "Stand up," he said, "I am only a man myself."* [34]

> *"They love to be greeted in the marketplaces and to have men*

---

[34]Acts 10:25-26. See also Rev. 19:10 for a sobering reminder that "only fools rush in where angels fear to tread."

211

call them 'Rabbi.' But you are not to be called 'Rabbi,' for you have only one Master and you are all brothers. And do not call anyone on earth 'father,' for you have one Father, and he is in heaven. Nor are you to be called 'teacher,' for you have one Teacher, the Christ. The greatest among you will be your servant." [35]

This is why I write these things when I am absent, that when I come I may not have to be harsh in my use of authority—the authority the Lord gave me for building you up, not for tearing you down. [36]

*Paul, a servant [**doulos:** bondslave] of Christ Jesus....* [37]

There are enough forces arrayed against the body of Christ in this world; Christ's members must not seek to devour and destroy one another in competing for places of prestige in the body! Let us rather follow the example of the true Head, Jesus Christ: a Head who washed dirty feet and gave Himself up to redeem the whole body, even its most unseemly members.

If you and I were as committed to the body of Christ as is Jesus, the Head, what attitudes would we cultivate in order to build up that body? How would we think of, and behave toward, one another so as to display and develop a body of believers committed to glorifying God by serving one another?

If covenant, community, communion, and commitment are ever going to become a reality, there must be a change of attitude regarding love and patience, adoration and thankfulness, as well as approval and acceptance.

---

[35]Matt. 23:7-11.   [36]2 Cor. 13:10.   [37]Rom. 1:1.

Acceptance: "As God In Christ...."

Christlikeness in action and attitude toward one another is the key to building up the body of Christ. We must see our fellow body members through the eyes of our one Lord, Jesus Christ. In Christ, God has extended loving acceptance to each Christian, regardless of his or her weaknesses, idiosyncracies, pecularities, problems, and moral failures.

Every Christian comes from a tainted past and an inadequate present when he is added to the body of Christ. God's grace positions him in Christ's righteousness and begins to transform him into the full-grown likeness of Christ. But this process of spiritual growth (which began when first we turned to God as He came to us in the gospel of Christ, and will continue at least as long as you and I live on earth) is founded on God's "just as I am" acceptance of us in Christ.

Modern secular psychology has likewise come to the conclusion that all personal growth begins at the ground level of self-acceptance. As children, we find (or, sadly, fail to find) a basis of self-worth in the response of our parents, and later, of our peers. In Christ, we no longer base our self-acceptance on the opinions and evaluations of other people (however important and dear they may be to us), *but on God's acceptance of us in Christ.* However, we are still social creatures, and seek confirmation and reinforcement of our Father's loving acceptance in the eyes of our brothers and sisters in Christ:

> *Be kind and compassionate to one another, forgiving each other, just as in Christ God forgave you. Be imitators of God, therefore, as dearly loved children and live a life of love, just*

213

as Christ loved us and gave himself up for us as a fragrant offering and sacrifice to God.[38]

Accept one another, then, just as Christ accepted you, in order to bring praise to God.[39]

Accept him whose faith is weak, without passing judgment on disputable matters.[40]

This last passage reminds us that older brothers and sisters have a special relationship to the less mature siblings who look up to them for some confirmation of acceptance and a sense of "belonging" in the family of God. Older brothers and sisters can behave in such a way as to imply that acceptance in the family depends, not on the Father's gracious approval of each child in Christ, but on younger children conforming to the expectations of older children. The legitimate role of the mature Christian leader as an example for the weaker Christian is thus perverted:

Be careful, however, that the exercise of your freedom does not become a stumbling block to the weak. For if anyone with a weak conscience sees you who have this knowledge eating in an idol's temple, won't he be emboldened to eat what has been sacrificed to idols? So this weak brother, for whom Christ died, is destroyed by your knowledge. When you sin against your brothers in this way and wound their weak conscience, you sin against Christ.[41]

When Peter came to Antioch, I opposed him to his face, because he was in the wrong. Before certain men came from James, he used to eat with the Gentiles. But when they arrived, he began to draw back and separate himself from the Gentiles because he was afraid of those who belonged to the

---

[38]Eph. 4:32-5:2.   [39]Rom. 15:7.
[40]Rom. 14:1.   [41]1 Cor. 8:9-12.

214

circumcision group. The other Jews joined him in his hypocrisy, so that by their hypocrisy even Barnabas was led astray.[42]

Older Christian: What are you really teaching your younger brothers and sisters about the basis of a man's or woman's acceptance before God? Beware of mixed signals: "Actions speak louder than words." Our words may teach the truth of the gospel, but the tone of our voices, the look on our faces, and the power of our example can shout down the truth and proclaim a "no gospel" instead. There is more than one way to proclaim the truth of the gospel, and more than one way to pervert it:

> *So whether you eat or drink or whatever you do, do it all for the glory of God. Do not cause anyone to stumble, whether Jews, Greeks or the church of God—even as I try to please everybody in every way. For I am not seeking my own good but the good of many, so that they may be saved. Follow my example, as I follow the example of Christ.*[43]

Approval: Without Threat Or Intimidation

The truth of the gospel demands that God's children recognize and rejoice in one anothers' freedom to serve in the body of Christ according to the unique measure of grace and faith that He has given to each member.[44] Your ministry cannot be a carbon copy of mine, nor should it be. My place in the body of Christ does not exist to measure up to your expectations, nor yours to mine. Both you and your ministry are God's gift to me and to the rest of the body of Christ, and it is the height of folly to look a gift horse in the mouth when God is the giver.

---

[42]Gal. 2:11-13.   [43]1 Cor. 10:31-11:1.
[44]See Rom. 12:1-8; 1 Cor. 12; Eph. 4:1-16; 1 Peter 4:10-11.

The church which Paul had planted at Corinth was reprimanded by the Spirit of God for dividing into cliques and parties. Each "elite group" failed to appreciate the others' contribution to the whole body that God Himself had assembled at the cost of Christ's blood: Paulites despising those of Apollos, Apollosites despising Cephasites, and those who presumed to be exclusively "of Christ" no doubt looking down on all the rest.[45]

Prophets and tongues-speakers competed with each other, and among themselves, for attention to their gifts in the assembly.[46] Each bickering faction probably fancied itself the "in group," the elite, and in so doing, held a judgement of disapproval toward all the others. "What could she possibly know about the matter? She learned everything she knows from Peter's crowd." "Those prophets are such a bunch of know-it-alls. What we really need is less of them and more praise in tongues."

Let's give each other the time and space we all need to grow to maturity in whatever place the Lord assigns us in the body of Christ. Each of us has silly quirks, hang-ups, customs, cultural peculiarities, personal "likes" and "dislikes," as well as odd habits. God called each of us to minister His grace to other members of the body of Christ, and He has called us as gum poppers, fingernail biters, hair twirlers, boisterous extroverts, sensitive artistic types, sentimental emotionalists, hard-headed rationalists, country bumpkins, and city slickers. No doubt, we all have much that God will need to change after we are added to the body,

---

[45]See 1 Cor. 1-3.
[46]See 1 Cor. 12-14.

but that is the business of each disciple and his Lord. We are not called to make one another over into our own image by threatening, intimidating, and self-righteously criticizing one another.

Non-Critical Attitude: Not Judgmental

God can use one Christian to help another reach his or her potential as a minister-member of the body of Christ, but only when the log of self-centeredness is no longer coming between one's own eye and his brother's life. We must deliberately trade the log of self-righteousness for the cross of God's righteousness.[47] I can (and must) receive my brother, with no qualifications or misgivings, on the same basis that God receives both him and me: *the cross of Christ.*

The body is Christ's, not mine. With His own blood He bought each member; by His gospel, He called each member; according to His grace and wisdom He sets each member in place. To have no use for one's brother or sister, and whatever gift(s) each one contributes to the whole body, leaves one with an embarrassing problem: How could he be of Christ, but not of me, if I am a Christian? Why would Christ have a place for her (and her talents) in His body, when I have no place for her in my heart? Truly, the judgement one directs to his brother or sister is measured out again to oneself. It is the judgmental, censorious spirit that is out of place in the body, not one's brother.

It goes without saying that persistent, unrepented sin is a cancer not to be trifled with in the body of Christ. After a

---

[47]See Matt. 7:1-5 and compare Matt. 5:20; Rom. 2:1-29.

first and second admonition fails, and the sinning member refuses to hear even the church through its proper spokesmen, there must be a clear and definite recognition that the member cut off from Christ is also cut off from the life of the body. In a previous section, I have discussed this painful situation.[48]

The amputation of a diseased member is sometimes necessary to protect the health of the rest of the body, but (I speak with reverence) Christ is not a masochist. He does not want His body members assuming the role of Great Physician and performing any unauthorized amputations or radical surgeries on other members of His body. I cannot approve of everything you may believe or do as a member of Christ's body, nor can you always give me "across the board" agreement. I cannot even agree with certain things that I believed and did as a Christian ten years ago. We are all changing—hopefully, growing and maturing toward greater conformity to Christ. If we are not changing, this is a sign of sickness, not health.

A deposit of *unchanging gospel truth,* firmly retained, provides the Christian with a firm base on which to stand, build, and grow for the rest of his or her life. We are free to jettison any spoiled cargo we may find aboard the ship of faith, but the anchor of the gospel and the compass of God's revealed Word must never be thrown overboard. The "deep truths of the faith" must be held to "with a clear conscience"; the truth about Christ and His redemptive death,

---

[48]See Part 1, *The Love of Christ in the Local Congregation,* pp. 20-22, 86-87.

burial, and resurrection must never be surrendered or compromised:

Some have rejected these and so have shipwrecked their faith.[49]

If we refuse to stand for something (the truth of the gospel), we will be ready to fall for anything.[50] On the other hand, if we attempt to anchor Christ's fleet with the weight of legalistic requirements and steer by an extra-biblical (or non-biblical) compass, however useful and reliable these may seem to us, we will collide with one another and sink into egocentric oblivion long before our vessels reach the heavenly home port.

Who are you to judge someone else's servant? To his own master he stands or falls. And he will stand, for the Lord is able to make him stand.[51]

Adoration And Thankfulness To God

God accepts each of us *as we are,* and we need each other *as we are.* If we insist on a "perfect or nothing" relationship with one another, then we will have *nothing!* I trust that our natural families are not based on "perfect or nothing." We

[49]1 Tim. 1:19. Compare 2 Tim. 2:16-18; Gal. 1:6-10; 2:5; 1 Cor. 15:1-4f; Col. 1:21-23; 2:6-23; 1 John 4:1-6; 2 John 7-9.
[50]Note Eph. 4:14f.
[51]Rom. 14:4. See also Paul's First Epistle to Timothy, which takes as its theme the importance of a "sincere faith" which holds firmly to "the mystery of godliness" in all "good conscience." Paul repeatedly refers here to some who would impose teachings on the family of God which have nothing to do with the apostolic gospel. Timothy is warned to oppose the influence of these men and their teaching, and to guard his own heart against their corrupt emphases and motives.

believe in one another, accept one another, and are thankful for the participation of each member of the family *just as each is*. If the mother overcooks a meal, if the father is late getting home from work, if the children have a fight or fail to clean their rooms, what do we do?

Hopefully, we accept what could not be helped, forgive human weakness, discuss disputable points, and discipline both ourselves and our children where persistent irresponsibility or deliberate rebellion are obvious.

We do not *give up* on one another, nor do we *reject* any family member and what he or she *can* contribute, simply because our personal expectations were not met. Rather, Christian families will thank God and adore Him in recognition of His gifts and talents in each family member. Likewise, in the wider Christian community, each member and each member's ministry should be viewed as God's gift to the whole community. Blessed is the congregation whose members really understand this truth, and respond by falling down before our gracious heavenly Father in thanks and praise for each brother and each sister.[52]

How often we have failed to give honor to whom honor is due, and to give supreme honor to Him from whom all good things flow! Every member of the body of Christ is a minister, and no ministry is meaningless or valueless when done in Christ's name.

"And if anyone gives a cup of cold water to one of these little

---

[52]Note carefully Rom. 1:8-12; 1 Cor. 1:4-9; 2 Cor. 9:12-15; Phil. 1:3-8; Col. 1:3-6; 1 Thess. 1:2-3; 2 Thess. 1:3-4.

*ones because he is my disciple, I tell you the truth, he will
certainly not lose his reward."* [53]

Those quiet, beautiful spirits who serve the Lord Jesus in
their daily, plodding walk of faith are really priests and
priestesses offering spiritual sacrifices to God through the
great High Priest, Jesus Christ. It is past time that we recognize one another for who we really are, and give glory to
God for one another's ministries, however menial or lowly
some may appear to the fleshly eye.

Remember, a Galilean peasant-preacher washing dirty feet
is presented to us as the incarnation of God. If we believe
this, surely we can believe that the man who cleans a latrine
or the woman who wipes dirty noses is a minister.

Love And Patience

Of all the attitudes to which God is calling us in order to
express and develop the biblical concept of community,
love and patience are the most crucial. Christ is building
His church; it cannot be done in the weakness of human
flesh. The fruit of the one Spirit, by whom we all were baptized into one body, must flow out of our hearts and embrace the whole community of believers. We will seek and
find innumerable excuses to reject one another and to set
ourselves apart from our brothers and sisters unless we continue to grow in the patient love of Christ.

If we are growing together in His love, we will be patient
and longsuffering toward one another, for His love is pa-

---

[53]Matt. 10:42. Compare Matt. 25:40.

221

tient, pure-hearted, peaceable, and gentle.[54] In a world rife with broken families, broken commitments, and broken people, may the Christian community shine forth as a united body of many members with differing characteristics, backgrounds, and abilities, holding faithfully to Christ and ministering God's healing grace to one another.

---

[54] See 1 Cor. 13:4-13; Rom. 12:9-21; 13:8-10; 14:1-15:7.

13

THE MEANING OF MEMBERSHIP IN THE BODY OF CHRIST

Among the most profound of all written literature, ancient and modern, Paul's letter to the Ephesians towers like a colossus.[55]

---

[55]Because the words "in Ephesus" do not follow Paul's greeting to the saints in three of our most ancient and important manuscript sources, some have concluded that the epistle we call "Ephesians" was actually an encyclical, or general epistle, intended for circulation among various local churches (perhaps in Asia Minor). This is a point of considerable debate among New Testament scholars, but is of questionable value to most students. I mention it only to point out that the authority of the epistle derives, not from its original recipients, but from its apostolic author, Paul. Although it is now fashionable in some circles to deny that Paul wrote this letter (as also the Pastorals), the church has always received it as a genuinely apostolic document, and no textual evidence opposes Pauline authorship, as even such a liberal scholar as William Barclay acknowledged. For convenience, I will herein refer to the epistle by its commonly accepted title, "Ephesians."

Even in its own element, among the divinely inspired documents of the New Testament, it is arguably preeminent in its rich and lofty exposition of the meaning of Christ. The letter has to do with God's purpose "from before the foundation of the world," the Almighty's wisdom concerning redemption in Jesus Christ, and His will concerning relationships in the body of Christ. Paul also deals with the church's warfare against spiritual forces of wickedness in the world as she awaits the return of her divine Husband. To catch a glimpse of Paul's concept of the church as the body of Christ in its cosmic significance, we could hardly do better than a consideration of Paul's Ephesian letter, and its sister letter to the Colossians:

> *And God placed all things under [Christ's] feet and appointed him to be head over everything for the church, which is his body, the fullness of him who fills everything in every way.*[56]

> *And [Christ] is the head of the body, the church; he is the beginning and the firstborn from among the dead, so that in everything he might have the supremacy. For God was pleased to have all his fullness dwell in him, and through him to reconcile to himself all things, whether things on earth or things in heaven by making peace through his blood, shed on the cross.*[57]

One Body, One Gospel, One Spirit

The church is the covenant people of God, now "come of age." It is the fruition of the eternal purpose which God has been working in the history of Israel (in a unique way) and

---

[56]Eph. 1:22-23; 2:15-16; 3:6; 4:4, 11-12, 16; 5:23, 29-30.
[57]Col. 1:18-20. See also Col. 1:24; 2:19; 3:15.

in the history of all nations. Someday—a day known only to the Father—the fruit will be fully ripened and the harvest gathered in. In the meantime, the church lives in a fallen world as the salt and light of God's presence and kingly power. God's covenant people have a stewardship and mission of the highest importance: to proclaim and embody the Good News of the kingdom of God in the midst of a corrupt and dying generation, so that every person who seeks life and light and truth may be drawn to the lifted up Christ for salvation and transformation into His image.

Each local congregation or community of Christians is a localized expression of this sublime purpose of God. The Christian community is to represent and affirm the kingly rule of God in Christ, as the Lord Himself did in His incarnation. The church is the "new incarnation," the body of Christ among men and women. Indwelt by His Spirit of love and holiness, each member of the body responds to the authority of the Head—Christ Himself. The Spirit who dwells in the body of Christ and its several members is that promised Helper, Counselor, Comforter, and Teacher who was to come into the world as Christ's representative.[58] Through the Holy Spirit, Christ guides and energizes His body as it continues His redemptive mission in the world.[59]

---

[58]Note carefully John 14:15-27; 15:26-27; 16:12-15.

[59]See Acts 1:1. Luke's subject in his "former book" (Gospel of Luke) was "all that Jesus *began* to do and to teach until the day He was taken up to heaven." His second work (Acts) has been rightly described as an account of what Jesus *continued* to do and to teach through the Holy Spirit in the church, from the day of Pentecost. His work in and through His body *continues* by the Holy Spirit,

225

But as access to the Father comes only through the Son, and access to the Son only through the Spirit who inspired the Scriptures and indwells the church, so also access to the Spirit comes only through faith in the gospel entrusted to the apostles. It is in their role as witnesses to the Risen Christ and stewards of the revealed mysteries of the Kingdom that the apostles will always have authority in the church.[60] We have no access to the truth of the gospel except through them. The apostles are therefore the "inner core" of the Christian community through whom we have access to the authentic Christ, the authentic gospel, and the authentic Spirit. They speak today with authority in the New Testament and through every Christian who stands on their teaching. Any Jesus differing from the apostles' is "another Jesus"; "another Jesus" can only be the subject of "another gospel"; "another gospel" cannot but impart "another spirit."

"My prayer is not for them [the apostles-L.D.] alone. I pray also for those who will believe in me through their message."[61]

For if someone comes to you and preaches a Jesus other than the Jesus we preached, or if you receive a different spirit from

although the working of the Spirit in the church today need not be a *duplication* of every first-century phenomenon. Similarly, although Paul's sufferings for the gospel were a *continuation* of Christ's own sufferings, they were not a *duplication*. The "atonement" aspect of suffering was completed by Christ. See Col. 1:24. Compare Acts 9:4.

[60]See Matt. 19:28; John 17:20; Acts 1:15-26; 1 Cor. 4:1, 9-17; 9:1-2; 14:36-38; 2 Cor. 10:8; 11:4-6, 13-15; 12:11-12; 13:10; Gal. 1-2; Eph. 2:19-20; 3:2-9; 1 John 1:1-4; 4:1-6; 2 John 7-11; 1 Peter 1:10-12; 2 Peter 1:16-21; Rev. 21:14.

[61]John 17:20. Compare John 20:24-31; 21:24; Luke 1:1-4; 1 Cor. 15:1-11; 1 John 1:4.

the one you received, or a different gospel from the one you accepted, you put up with it easily enough.[62]

But we ought always to thank God for you, brothers loved by the Lord, because from the beginning God chose you to be saved through the sanctifying work of the Spirit and through belief in the truth. He called you to this through our gospel, that you might share in the glory of our Lord Jesus Christ. So then, brothers, stand firm and hold to the teachings we passed on to you, whether by word of mouth or by letter.[63]

A strong Christian community must be built on the solid foundation of the apostolic gospel, through which alone we all have access into the one body by one Spirit.[64]

One Head, Many Members

An international credit card company makes use of the advertising slogan, "Membership has its privileges." In the matter of belonging to the body of Christ, one must add, "...and its responsibilities." Belonging to Jesus (the Head) means belonging to His body, a truth I have examined in depth in the preceding section subtitled *Members One Of Another.* Those who individually answer the call of Christ's gospel and submit themselves to Him as Lord and Savior are no longer simply individuals; they are now *individual members* of Christ. Belonging to Him, they belong to one another. This reality explains why the New Testament presents over sixty specific admonitions to express "one another-ness" as members of Christ's body.[65]

---

[62]2 Cor. 11:4. Compare Gal. 3:1-5; 2 John 9.
[63]2 Thess. 2:13-15. Compare Col. 1:13-14; 1 Peter 2:9-10.
[64]Note Eph. 2:14-18; 1 Cor. 12:13.
[65]Some of these "one another" admonitions are listed in an appendix to this book.

I am convinced that God loves diversity. Within the unity of His Being, there is the plurality of Persons, the "Otherness" of Father, Son, and Holy Spirit. A look at the universe God created confirms this point: He didn't make one basic style of tree, one type of flower, one design of bird. Even among creatures of the same species, individual differences between each specimen are observable. He made each of us with different faces, different temperaments, personalities, and abilities.

Man tends to copy and clone; God creates diversity, and calls it "very good." I have heard some people object to the concept of unity in diversity; they don't believe it can exist. To such people, diversity and individuality among members of the body of Christ are a threat to unity. But seriously consider the fact that God creates each of us in all our personal uniqueness, and calls us *as individuals* to be joined to Christ and one another:

> *Just as each of us has one body with many members, and these members do not all have the same function, so in Christ we who are many form one body, and each member belongs to all the others. We have different gifts, according to the grace given us.*[66]

Egoism hates all that is not a mere colony or extension of the "self"; selfism denies that one individual's welfare can coincide with the good of another. It is the kingdom of darkness that prefers envy and competition to love and cooperation. In order to believe in love at all, we must learn to *enjoy* what differs from the self. Because we tend toward sinful self-centeredness, we find it difficult to conceive of

---

[66]Rom. 12:4-6.

any "self" that is humble, loving, and benevolent rather than proud, egocentric, and grasping.

Some have even thought of God as some sort of Cosmic Egomaniac, a Supreme Self-Centeredness who makes arbitrary demands of obedience and worship on creatures whom He made in His own image because He really only wanted to worship Himself through them! But when we come to know God as He has come to us in the Person of Jesus Christ, such blasphemous lies and misconceptions seem ridiculous. Whoever heard of an egomaniac who so desired to save the lives of his enemies that he would allow himself to be brutally murdered by them? A self-centered God is a contradiction in terms. He gave us our lives, our freedom, and our individuality; we foolishly allowed ourselves to be conned out of them.

God then gave His own Son, His very Heart, to win back for us what Satan had stolen. To worship this God is to adore Love, Truth, Holiness, Righteousness, and Mercy; to despise Him is to embrace the slavery of self-centeredness, sin, and death. This God swears oaths in His own Name because there is no one greater by whom to swear;[67] He desires and deserves our obedience because there is no greater Object for man to worship. All other loyalties must either be subordinate to God or idolatrous, not because He is egotistical, but because He alone is supremely worthy. With these preliminary understandings, we can begin to consider the purposes for which God ordained the church, the body of Christ.

---

[67]See Heb. 6:13f.

The Primary Purpose: To Be Transformed
Into Christ's Image

The body of Christ exists on earth so that the redeeming presence of Christ may continue in the world through His Spirit, who dwells in the whole body collectively, and in each member individually. The Spirit works in and through the several body members to progressively transform each one into the spiritual image of Christ. The interaction of members must be such as will permit the expression of the life of the Spirit among them; the forms utilized by the community must allow the body to function as a *living organism.*

The various members draw spiritual nourishment from the Spirit of Christ as He works through each member's ministry. This process is called "mutual edification." As Christ fed the multitudes through a meager offering placed in His hands by a child's faith and distributed by His obedient disciples, so would His Spirit now nourish His body. As each member places his or her life at Christ's disposal, the Spirit makes much of our little and uses our gifts to nourish other members of the body. The result of nourishment is, of course, health and growth; the goal or standard toward which the whole body is growing together is each member's spiritual maturity:

> *But to each one of us grace has been given as Christ apportioned it....It was he who gave some to be apostles, some to be prophets, some to be evangelists, and some to be pastors and teachers, to prepare God's people for works of service, so that the body of Christ may be built up until we all reach unity in the faith and in the knowledge of the Son of God and be-*

come mature, attaining to the whole measure of the fullness of Christ. Then we will no longer be infants, tossed back and forth by the waves, and blown here and there by every wind of teaching and by the cunning and craftiness of men in their deceitful scheming. Instead, speaking the truth in love, we will in all things grow up into him who is the Head, that is, Christ. From him the whole body, joined and held together by every supporting ligament, grows and builds itself up in love, as each part does its work.[68]

God never intended Christ's disciples to live and grow in isolation, to face the world alone as separate entities. Christ stabilizes us and binds us together as members of His one body. He Himself is the ground of truth in which our lives are rooted, as well as the source of light toward which we grow. Together, we reach for the Son, not competitively but cooperatively; not by selfishly grasping but by lovingly surrendering to Christ and (in Him) to one another.

Outside the body of Christ, we were completely at the mercy of the howling winds of worldly philosophies and ideologies. In Christ, we stand on immovable truth and acknowledge one Lord, Jesus Christ. He alone is our absolute standard and goal. Therefore, the body of Christ is a kind of counterculture which stands in contrast and opposition to this world's moral relativism, speculative philosophies, and bankrupt values. Caesar was wrong in persecuting Christians as political subversives and enemies of the state, but was right in viewing the church as a threat to Rome's blasphemies, decadence, and corruption. There are still places in the world today where the church is watched suspiciously and even persecuted openly. The body of Christ should be

---

[68]Eph. 4:7, 11-16. See also Rom. 8:28-30; 12:1-8.

as conspicuous in a decadent society as salt in bland food or light in a dark room! To be ignored is a rebuke; to be patronized is an insult; to be honored by a system of evil is a death knell.

"If the world hates you, keep in mind that it hated me first. If you belonged to the world, it would love you as its own. As it is, you do not belong to the world, but I have chosen you out of the world. That is why the world hates you. Remember the words I spoke to you: 'No servant is greater than his master.' If they persecuted me, they will persecute you also. " [69]

The world has not become less "worldly" since Christ spoke these words; rather, the modern church has all too often become less Christlike, less "Christian." Yet, the very purpose for which the church exists in the world is that it might stand apart from the world by bearing the image of Christ.

*The Secondary Purpose: To Be Edified
By Each Member's Ministry Of Love*

The body of Christ bears witness to Him in the world by each member's embodiment of Christ in relationship to the whole body, which (in turn) stands in relationship to the world. Political ideologists argue about whether the state exists to serve the individual, or the individual to serve the state. The love of Christ at work in the body of believers makes such arguments seem irrelevant: *the Christian community exists to serve the individual member, even as the individual member exists to serve the body.*

---

[69]John 15:18-20. Compare 1 John 3:1, 11-17; 4:1-6; 5:19-21; Matt. 5:10-12; 2 Tim. 3:12; 1 Peter 4:12-17; Rev. 2-3.

The body grows as its members grow, and its individual members grow by giving to and receiving from the body that which God has entrusted to each member. As each member's personal individuality is unique, so is each member's contribution to the character and growth of the whole community. The primary objective of the body is each member's transformation into the Christ's likeness; the secondary objective (inseparable from the primary, and subservient to it) is that each member contribute to the building up of the whole body by expressing its individual uniqueness of abilities, talents, gifts, and ministries.

It is at this point that the modern church has most obviously departed from the biblical norm. There is an almost universal but unspoken belief among Christians that the man who stands before the congregation to proclaim the word of God or to preside over the assembly is "the minister," and the rest of the church is composed of spectators. Some churches have carried this error to more obvious extremes than others, but I know of few churches where the misconception is not deeply rooted, and fewer still where any deliberate measures are being taken to correct it.

Each member of the body of Christ has a ministry; each one is a minister, a servant of the church. Each one has abilities that the others lack, and which the whole body needs. Members of the body of Christ are specialists, doing what no one else in the body can do, supplying what no other member can supply. The growth of the whole community depends on each member's ministry:

> *We have different gifts, according to the grace given us. If a man's gift is prophesying, let him use it in proportion to his faith. If it is serving, let him serve; if it is teaching, let him*

teach; if it is encouraging, let him encourage; if it is contributing to the needs of others, let him give generously; if it is leadership, let him govern diligently; if it is showing mercy, let him do it cheerfully.[70]

Our entire lives are rendered acceptable to God as they are offered to Him by faith in Christ.[71] Everything we think, say, and do is to be offered "in Christ's name," as His disciples. Christ has deputized the members of His body; He has given them authority to carry out His works in His Spirit, as His representatives on earth. But He has also entrusted each deputy-member with his or her own specific and unique ministry.

We all answer to the same King, we all serve under Him in the same kingdom, but your particular territory is not the same as mine. Each of us will give account to the Lord concerning our own particular stewardship, not another's. Whatever our personal abilities may be, they are given to us by God's grace; you and I are responsible to activate and express those gifts according to the measure of faith God has given us individually.

God's grace is the source of each member's gifts and abilities, and the faith that He bestows determines the particular shape and capacity of each member's ministry to the body.

-----

[70]Rom. 12:6-8. (See the entire context of Rom. 12, and compare also 1 Cor. 12:4-6, 12-31; 1 Peter 4:10-11.) According to Paul, the gospel of Christ sets us free from the slavery of sin and death by enjoining upon us slavery to Christ. This new relationship is to be expressed with the same wholehearted devotion that had characterized our obedience to sin. Our entire being and all of our gifts are now placed at Christ's disposal and are sanctified (set apart) and revitalized by His Holy Spirit. See Rom. 6-8.

[71]See Rom. 12:1-2; 1 Cor. 10:31-11:1; Col. 3:17; Heb. 13:15-16.

He creates the vessel, and He fills it. Each vessel renders back to the Creator the gift it has received by freely and lovingly pouring itself out to serve and nourish the other body members. To wash the feet of a body member is to wash the feet of Christ, the Head. Worshipping God and serving the body of Christ are as inseparably bound together as the first and second great commandments: loving God (whom we cannot see) and loving man (who is made in God's image).

Each member's ministry is vital to the growth of the body (Christian community). Yet, in my years of addressing Christian communities and counseling Christian individuals, most with whom I have spoken could not answer the question, "What is your ministry?" Christ's church seems to be in the grip of a major identity crisis. Collectively, we seem not to know that we are the body of Christ; individually, we seem not to know our place in the body. A careful reading of the main New Testament texts addressing these matters clearly shows that *outside* the body of Christ, we are lost; *inside,* we are at home![72]

Apart from Christ, our lives are adrift and our personalities unfulfilled. In Christ, we find meaning and fulfillment. Yet, how few churches really reflect this reality; how few Chris-

---

[72]See Rom. 12:1-21; 1 Cor. 12:1-31; Eph. 2:1-22; 4:4-6:9; Col. 3:5-4:6; Titus 2:11-14. Each of these texts contains a strong "before" and "after" emphasis, referring not merely to personal alienation from God, but also to reconciliation to God in a redeemed society, or body. The Spirit of Christ, who animates this "body," also transforms all the social relationships of each member. There is to be no aspect of the Christian's new life which is unrelated to Christ, untouched by the Spirit. Every relationship is spiritual, every responsibility a ministry.

tians experience this truth! Christian brother, take comfort! Sister in the Lord, be of good cheer! By God's grace, learn a truth that can set you free to know who you really are and to become all that God wants to make of you. Please take this to heart, and let no one rob you of your joy in this matter: *your gift to the body of Christ is you yourself!* There is a space in the body of Christ that is shaped exactly like you, a place that can be filled only with your unique, redeemed individuality. Your ministry is not essentially "what you do"; it is *who you are right now,* by the grace of God.[73] And by His grace, it is an acceptable offering to the Lord, and well pleasing in His sight.

---

[73]See 1 Cor.15:10; compare Rom.12:6-8; 1 Cor.12:27-30; Eph.3:2-3; 4:11; 1 Peter 4:10-11. A careful comparison of these passages will reveal two aspects of divine grace: first, God's grace to the individual in equipping him or her with unique gifts, talents, and privileges (including redemption in Christ); second, God's grace to the body in placing these redeemed, gifted individuals in a relationship of mutual ministry to other redeemed, gifted individuals for the building up of the whole body. In this second sense (at least), a Christian's individuality is inseparable from his role in the body of Christ: what God has made each member to be is the same as the ministry he (or she) is to express in relation to the other body members. Let teachers teach; let contributors give generously; let leaders govern diligently; let those who show mercy do so cheerfully. The list could be extended indefinitely. To ask, "What is my ministry?" is essentially to ask, "Who am I, in Christ Jesus?" And *in* Christ, we are the same individuals we were *outside* of Christ, with one major difference: our whole being is now turned to the service of God and motivated by His loving Holy Spirit. Peter and John were still fishermen after their call—only now, they were fishers of men. Paul was still a rabbi, but now in the service of Jesus. The "newness" of one's life in Christ refers to spiritual position and moral direction, not personal individuality.

Functioning As A Covenant Community

How does the Christian community function, in a practical way, so as to fulfill its purpose of transforming each member into the image of Christ by means of mutual ministry?

First, there must be a submission of all community members to a covenant relationship as "members one of another" under the headship of Christ. We must see ourselves as vitally related to one another because we are members of the same body. If I believe I am too insignificant to matter in the body, I am wrong; if I believe I am so spiritually superior and self-sufficient as to have no need of other members, I am equally wrong:

> *If the foot should say, "Because I am not a hand, I do not belong to the body," it would not for that reason cease to be part of the body....The eye cannot say to the hand, "I don't need you!" And the head cannot say to the feet, "I don't need you!"* [74]

In the body of Christ, we belong to one another, because we belong to Christ and He has given us to one another. I am both a gift and a responsibility to you, as you are to me. This is true in the broad, universal sense, but the Bible clearly presents a practical, day by day application of the "members one of another" principle. This is possible only in the context of the local church (or Christian community) where members have a stated understanding of, and commitment to, a covenant relationship of loving submission to one another as members of the body of Christ.

---

[74]1 Cor. 12:15, 21.

In modern western civilization, we have overcompensated for some of the shortcomings of the ancient oriental emphasis on "community solidarity." If the ancient east overshadowed the significance of the individual by exalting the claims of society, the modern west has despised responsibility to the community and made each individual the measure of all things.

We live in our own separate boxes, from which we emerge each morning to climb into our rolling metal boxes. We drive up to a fast food box and grab a boxed breakfast. We arrive at the box where we work, spend the day in our personal cubical, drive back home to our private box, and catch a little news and entertainment on the television box.

I have (barely) exaggerated to make a point: In the world, we are encouraged to ignore other people, to avoid involvement with others (beyond certain superficialities necessary for personal survival). In Christ, we are commanded to give up the absolute claims of self, to feed Christ's sheep and tend His lambs with whatever gifts He has blessed us, and to be our brother's keeper. Unless we submit to a personal commitment on a local level, we will probably be content to love whoever we feel like loving, whenever we find it convenient to do so.

Second, there are certain concepts, realizations, and insights to which each member of the Christian community should be personally committed, and which each should constantly share with his or her fellow members. Among them:

1. *Understanding the nature and purpose of the church as the body of Christ,* and my personal rela-

tionship to each fellow member of the body (especially in the local Christian community).

2. *Identifying my God-given gift(s) and involving them in ministry to my fellow members of the body.* God's gracious gifts flow "naturally" from who we are in Christ; they are the ministries that we were designed by God to perform. The hand doesn't strain to function as a hand, because it was *designed* to so function.

3. *Developing my attitude* for using my gifts to serve the Lord's purposes. It is possible to mismanage one's stewardship by using gifts for self-serving ends. Everything done, in word or deed, should be a loving contribution to the building up of the body of Christ.

4. *Devoting and using my ministry for the good of the whole body.* We must avoid the errors of isolationism and individualism by deliberately contributing to the edification and growth of the whole (local) community of believers.

5. *Discovering ways in which to joyfully and lovingly express my gift(s).*

6. *Recognizing the contribution of my gift(s) and ministry* toward educating, edifying, and evangelizing. These three functions of the body of Christ are essential to the building up of the body in love, and all ministries and gifts within the body are related to these three objectives. When the body of Christ

functions as a Spirit-animated organism, its ministries will be seen to accomplish everything that the shouters and screamers among us are trying to embarrass or intimidate us into doing.

In Christian discipleship, "being" always precedes and motivates "doing." Love and compassion motivate and liberate; guilt and fear paralyze and enslave. We need not (and will not) always *enjoy* the specific tasks that are involved in fulfilling our ministries and in doing God's will. However, a bitter cup, accepted because we love the Lord and His body of believers, is the most pure expression of Christlikeness with which we can glorify God in this world.

7. *Realizing that there is no such thing as a "personal relationship with Jesus" without a personal relationship with His body, the church.*

> *Both the one who makes men holy and those who are made holy are of the same family. So Jesus is not ashamed to call them brothers. He says, "I will declare your name to my brothers...." And again he says, "Here am I, and the children God has given me."* [75]

We cannot say "yes" to Jesus while saying "no" to His blood-bought brothers and sisters. God offers us a "package deal" in Christ: all the gracious blessings that flow from Christ, the Head, together with all the blessings and responsibilities of belonging to

---

[75]Heb. 2:11-13. See also Heb. 3:6; 1 Tim. 3:15; Mark 3:35.

His body, the church. What we do (or fail to do) in relationship to the church is what we do (or fail to do) concerning Christ Himself.[76] There is no way to belong to the Head without being part of the body.

8. *Remembering that in the midst of a depersonalized world, one enters into an intimate, personal family relationship in the local Christian community.* This family is one in which the love, mercy, compassion, and forbearance of God in Christ must prevail. In Jesus Christ, God is our Father and we are His children together. We must accept one another as He has accepted each one of His adopted children. As He has given us time and space in which to grow and mature, so must we do for one another. The atmosphere in the local church family should be one of affirmation, acceptance, and patience with one another.

> *Accept one another, then, just as Christ accepted you, in order to bring praise to God.*[77]

The greatness of any Christian community depends upon the greatness of Christ's love in each member's heart. Let us cease to measure greatness by any other standard.

---

[76]See Heb. 13:3 (N.A.S.B.); Matt. 25:31-46; 1 John 4:20-21; James 3:9-10f; Acts 9:1-5.
[77]Rom. 15:7.

...Then, Jesus took the towel
And knelt to wash their dirty feet.
The mighty King of Kings
Began to teach them something
new:
That love begins with service
And leadership with love
And greatness starts
When others know you
As a slave of God!...[78]

[78]Keith and Sanna Luker, *True Greatness* ©1988.

14

THE PURPOSE OF GIFTS

There are those who are resigned to accept the present fractured, splintered state of the body of Christ as a necessary evil in a fallen world. Yet, Christ did not come in order to compromise with any evil, but rather to conquer it through the lifting up of divine love in His human body on the cross. The ongoing scandal of division among members of Christ's body is one of the "enemies" that will one day be put under the Lord's feet. In the meanwhile, how can members of the body of Christ complacently accept a situation which is so utterly opposed to the will of Christ?

"My prayer is not for [the apostles] alone. I pray also for those who will believe in me through their message, that all of them may be one, Father, just as you are in me and I am in you. May they also be in us so that the world may believe that you have sent me. I have given them the glory that you gave me, that they may be one as we are one: I in them and

243

you in me. May they be brought to complete unity to let the world know that you sent me and have loved them even as you have loved me." [79]

He Lives, He Loves, He Is Holy

Members of the body of Christ share in the life of the Father and the Son through the Spirit who dwells in them. The indwelling Spirit sets apart (sanctifies) the children of God from among all other people in the world, gradually transforming their lives into the likeness of Christ. The transforming presence of the Spirit in the lives of God's children is their guarantee that, in God's appointed time, they will enter into full possession of the kingdom promised them: incorruptible bodies in a redeemed universe, in which God rules without opposition.[80]Until that time, the church (body of Christ) lives on the earth as a continuing demonstration and testimony to the fact that

"...God so loved the world that he gave his one and only Son, that whoever believes in him shall not perish but have eternal life." [81]

---

[79]John 17:20-23. Read carefully 1 Cor. 1:10-15; Rom. 12:16; 15:1-7; 2 Cor. 13:11; Phil 1:27; 2:1-11; 4:2; 1 Peter 3:8; Acts 4:32 and compare Matt. 11:29; Eph. 4:1-6; 4:20-5:2; Col. 3:8-4:1; 1 Peter 5:5. The "one mindedness" is a deliberate adoption of Christ's attitude of humble, loving service toward all, and especially toward the family of believers.

[80]See Col. 1:12-23; Matt. 13:36-43 and compare Rom. 8:9-11, 15-25; 5:1-5; Eph. 1:13-14; 4:30; 1 Cor. 15:42-58; 2 Cor. 1:20-22; 4:16-5:5; 1 Peter 1:1-2; Gal. 3:2, 14; 4:6; 5:19-23.

[81]John 3:16.

Christ's desire is that His body on earth should be a continuation of His own life, to show, in the midst of this world, that God is present, that He loves human beings sufficiently to give Himself up entirely to rescue them, and that He is entirely holy, righteous, and pure. The church is to embody the reality of God's presence and power, His holiness and His love. The Christian community is meant to do this by its members mutually submitting to one another because of their love for Christ and for one another. In other words, salvation involves *redeemed relationships*. As the Son submits Himself to the Father and the Father glorifies His Son, an "extended family" of God comes into being. The members of this family submit themselves to certain social relationships which God has ordained, and this results in a unique community which *displays the excellencies of God in the midst of this fallen world while it stands utterly apart from its corrupt attitudes, values, and life-styles.*[82]

Since redeemed relationships are based on the eternal character and infinite wisdom of God, we should expect them to reflect a balance that will not appeal to fallen man's extremism; the kingdom of God is neither traditional chauvinism nor radical liberationism. God's kingdom will be misunderstood, misrepresented, and rejected by both the secular "left" and secular "right" of this world's political system.

That is why the Christian community must be careful to maintain its own unique identity in the world, standing up

[82]See Matt. 5:10-16; Acts 26:17-18; Col. 1:12-14; 1 Peter 2:9-12.

for any cause that is right in the sight of God and opposing all that is anti-Christ. The body of Christ must never compromise itself by entirely identifying with any political movement, because in doing so it loses its own unique identity. We are to be "in this world, but not of this world."

Equality Of Position, Diversity Of Function

As Christians, we must be aware of the subtle divisive nature of a "left" or "right" philosophy; neither of these can ever permit the Lord's will regarding true unity through diversity to prevail.

The political left is quick to emphasize certain texts and features of New Testament theology that seem to portray Christ as a social revolutionary and the church as a socialist society: Christ ignored the conventions of the scribes and Pharisees in His treatment of women as full human beings with rights, dignity, and value. They were not to be lusted after as sex objects, nor acquired and discarded like cattle.[83]

The apostolic church seemed to ignore considerations of gender, race, social status, education, and economic class in its criteria of membership. Anyone who would obey the gospel of Jesus Christ was considered as much a member of the body as any other member, with the same access to God and to all spiritual blessings. Socialist economics and democratic egalitarianism are thus wrested "from Scripture."

---

[83]See Matt. 5:27-32; Mark 10:1-12; Luke 7:36-8:3; 16:16-18; John 4:27.

The political right is equally eager to seize and exploit any biblical teaching that seems to support resignation to the "establishment," however abusive and unjust the traditional system might be. The Bible is twisted into supporting the "divine right of kings," slavery, sexism, holy war, racism, and economic exploitation of the weak.

As might be expected, divine truth lies between these two ridiculous extremes. If the Bible affirms the right of private property (and I believe it does), it does so only on the condition that "owners" will see themselves as God's stewards and use His goods compassionately, to help those made in His image.[84]

If Scripture silences women and places them in submission to men in certain contexts (and it does), it also refers to female teachers, prophetesses, and perhaps even "deaconesses" in other settings.[85]

---

[84]Read 1 Tim. 6:17-19.

[85]Read Acts 18:24-26; 21:8-9; Rom. 16:1-3; 1 Tim. 3:11; 1 Cor. 11:4-6. The "silence of women in churches" should not be pulled out of its specific context: assemblies in which prophets were receiving divine revelation and other members were evaluating each prophecy. We simply cannot bind absolute silence on all women in assemblies of the body of Christ today on the basis of 1 Cor. 14:33-36. Will we forbid them to sing hymns with the rest of the congregation, or to openly participate in Bible classes? Likewise, the prohibition against women "teaching" and "exercising authority over a man" seems to be contextually restricted to the role of "elders" or "pastors": men are to be overseers of the local family of believers (1 Tim. 2:11-3:5; compare 1 Tim. 3:14-15). However, there are principles behind these prohibitions that require careful attention and application in today's churches.

If civil authorities are to be respected and obeyed when they fulfill their God-ordained function (and they are), they are also to be resisted and defied when they arrogate to themselves what belongs only to God.[86]

If slavery is not condemned outright in the New Testament, it is certainly transformed into something totally other than the secular institution when both slave and master together submit to Christ as Lord, and freedom from slavery to men is set forth as the ideal.[87]

In truth, both "Jesus, the socialist radical" and "Jesus, the right-wing reactionary" are poor caricatures of the living Christ presented to us in Scripture; each is indeed "another Jesus"! Similarly, the Christian community is neither a socialist state where individual identity is lost, nor a democracy where the majority rules, nor yet an aristocracy in which no person can rise above the level of his or her caste. *It is the body of Christ, in which each unique member submits to the authority of the Head for the well-being of the whole; it is the family of God in which all adopted children share equal status in the inheritance of the only begotten Son.*

There is true equality of position "in Christ"; but there is also submission to the order of the Father's household. God created us (male and female; Jew and Gentile), and reconciles us back to Himself and to one another in one body

---

[86]Read Acts 4:18-20; 5:27-29; Rev. 13:1-18; Dan. 3:1-18; 6:1-13; Exod. 1:15-21; 2 Kings 1.

[87]Read 1 Cor. 7:20-24; Philemon 15-16; Eph. 6:9; Col. 4:1.

248

through Christ's cross. Racial, cultural, sexual, and social class barriers are abolished in Christ. It is true that differences between the sexes were designed by God to create one "mankind" of two distinct halves, and that God's intention of distinct roles for the two halves of humanity will continue until that time when

"...people will neither marry nor be given in marriage; they will be like the angels in heaven." [88]

But it is equally true that in spiritual position, in human dignity, and in social status

...all of you who were baptized into Christ have clothed yourselves with Christ. There is neither Jew nor Greek, slave nor free, male nor female, for you are all one in Christ Jesus. [89]

Equality of position does not necessitate sameness of function or role. Still, there must be a visible demonstration in every Christian family (including the wider "church family") that the woman is not a "second-class citizen." Her status of submission to God's order of things in Christ should not be demeaning, degrading, or dehumanizing; rather, it should be redemptive, restorative, and revitalizing. Submission to Christ brings wholeness and personal fulfillment to men; it brings the same to women.

---

[88]Matt. 22:30.
[89]Gal. 3:27-28. Compare 1 Peter 3:7, where the distinctive nature of woman is acknowledged, but held in balance with her essential equality with man.

Different Gifts Build A United Body

The world longs for peace, brotherhood, and unity among the various cultures and nations of humanity. Its schemes to repair the breach in human relationships that began with the Fall of mankind in Eden are a dismal history of repeated failure. The Good News of the kingdom of God is an announcement that God has come, in the Person of Christ, to accomplish the work of reconciliation (restoring of fractured relationships) for which mere human power and ingenuity are utterly inadequate.[90] What man has failed to accomplish with his mighty striving, from the time of the Tower of Babel up to our modern United Nations, God has accomplished through the "weakness" of the cross of Christ!

Therefore, remember that formerly you who are Gentiles by birth and called "uncircumcised" by those who call themselves "the circumcision" (that done in the body by the hands of men)—remember that at that time you were separate from Christ, excluded from citizenship in Israel and foreigners to the covenants of the promise, without hope and without God in the world. But now in Christ Jesus you who were once far away have been brought near by the blood of Christ. For he himself is our peace, who has made the two one and has destroyed the barrier....His purpose was to create in himself one new man out of the two, thus making peace, and in this one body to reconcile both of them to God through the cross, by which he put to death their hostility. He came and preached peace to you who were far away [Gentiles-L.D.] and peace to those who were near [Jews-L.D.]. For through

---

[90]Read carefully Isa. 2:1-4; 9:6-7; Luke 1:76-79; 2:1-14.

him we both have access to the Father by one Spirit.[91]

*And they sang a new song: "You are worthy to take the scroll
and to open its seals, because you were slain, and with your
blood you purchased men for God from every tribe and language and people and nation."*[92]

Those who share life together "in Christ," being called out
of such diverse cultural backgrounds, often have little more
in common than the fact that they are God's chosen people,
purchased by the redemptive death and resurrection of
Christ, and sealed by the one Spirit:

*Make every effort to keep the unity of the Spirit through the
bond of peace. There is one body and one Spirit—just as you
were called to one hope when you were called—one Lord, one
faith, one baptism; one God and Father of all, who is over all
and through all and in all. But to each one of us grace has
been given as Christ apportioned it.*[93]

Unity is not an impossible ideal, nor is it to be attained by
the power of human flesh. It is a positional reality already
created by the Holy Spirit which is to be expressed and
maintained by the diligent practice of spiritual attitudes and
actions. For example, Jesus calls us to radically change our
entire mindset about such concepts as "greatness" and "authority":

---

[91]Eph. 2:11-18. Other passages that speak of the reconciliation of
the human family in Christ include Acts 2:38-39; John 10:14-17;
11:51-52; Rom. 1:16-17; 3:29-31; 4:9-12; 11:25-32; 15:8-12.
[92]Rev. 5:9. Compare Gen. 11:1-9; Acts 2:1-47.
[93]Eph. 4:3-7.

251

Jesus called them together and said, "You know that those who are regarded as rulers of the Gentiles lord it over them, and their high officials exercise authority over them. Not so with you. Instead, whoever wants to become great among you must be your servant, and whoever wants to be first must be slave of all. For even the Son of Man did not come to be served, but to serve, and to give his life as a ransom for many." [94]

Dr. Paul Brand and Philip Yancey have written a fascinating book in which the wonder of the human body is carefully compared with the wonder of the body of Christ (the church). They write:

The human body employs a bewildering zoo of cells, none of which, individually, resembles the larger body [i.e., the body as a whole-L.D.]. [95]

The authors go on to point out that their selection of the word "unlikely" (in describing the collection of parts that constitute the whole human body) is precisely the right word to convey the dissimilarities of the various parts: they are "unlike" one another. I personally was impressed with the appropriateness of the word "zoo," especially when the application is made to the church as the "body of Christ." Aren't we who are in Christ an amazingly diverse assortment of human specimens, coming out of a complex jungle of cultural, ethnic, economic, and religious backgrounds in response to the call of the gospel of Christ?

---

[94]Mark 10:42-45. See also Matt. 18:1-6; 23:1-12; Luke 22:24-30; John 13:1-17; compare how the Spirit applies the teaching in various relationships (e.g., Rom. 12:1-8; 1 Cor. 12:27-14:10; Eph. 5:21-30).

[95]Dr. Paul Brand and Philip Yancey, *Fearfully And Wonderfully Made* (Grand Rapids: Zondervan, 1980), p. 29.

Truly, the one Creator who made man's body from the dust of the earth is also the Redeemer who forms the body of Christ from the children of Adam and Eve who are scattered over the face of the whole earth. He calls each of us, as He called Abram. He breathes into the body of Christ, and into each member, the breath of life: His Spirit of holiness, love, liberty, and truth. The Spirit tames us, so that the lions among us can lie down peacefully with the lambs in this divine menagerie called "the church."

But the work of the Spirit, who brings order out of chaos, can be resisted. We can *grieve* the Spirit by hostile, malicious attitudes and behavior toward one another.[96] We can *quench* the dynamic energy of the Spirit at work among the body members by refusing to allow certain gifts to be expressed because of pride, prejudice, jealousy, and selfish ambition.[97]

Unfortunately, those who talk most emphatically about unity are often those who insist on having their own way! "Unity" to such people means "conformity to my personal preferences and opinions" (rather than to the word of God)

---

[96]See Eph. 4:29-32.

[97]See 1 Thess. 5:19-22. Compare 1 John 4:1-6; 1 Cor. 12:1-3; 13:8-10; 14:29. In applying Paul's injunction against "quenching the Spirit's fire" to spiritual gifts in general, I realize that I am going beyond Paul's immediate contextual application. I am not endorsing the claims of self-proclaimed modern day "prophets," since I believe that the church possesses a sufficient divine revelation in the Scriptures. I am simply saying that the work of the Spirit, who gives gifts to the body of Christ, is resisted when those gifts are not allowed free expression in a loving, orderly environment.

253

and "love" means "surrender to my demands" (instead of to Christ's lordship). Such "holy terrorists" do not understand that diversity is not opposed to love; it is *the only soil* in which love can grow, and *the only background* against which love's beauty can be displayed.

Brand and Yancey remind us that the human body is made of many different parts, none of which (by itself) resembles the whole. Paul applies this truth to the body of Christ, the Christian community. No single member is the ultimate standard or pattern for any other. Different parts that fit together in a complimentary, cooperative way cannot be cast from the same mold. Each member's embodiment of Christ is only partial, and needs balance and support from the whole body:

> *But in fact God has arranged the parts in the body, every one of them, just as he wanted them to be. If they were all one part, where would the body be? As it is, there are many parts, but one body.*[98]

Our common calling by the gospel of Christ, and the realities that we share in one body through responding faithfully to that calling, are the only foundations upon which human unity can stand. To seek elsewhere for common ground on which to build the body of Christ is to ignore God's clear revelation:

> *Consequently, you are no longer foreigners and aliens, but fellow citizens with God's people and members of God's household, **built on the foundation of the apostles and***

---

[98] 1 Cor. 12:18-20.

prophets, with Christ Jesus himself as the chief cornerstone.
In him the whole building is joined together and rises to be-
come a holy temple in the Lord. And in him you too are being
built together to become a dwelling in which God lives by his
Spirit.[99]

A Unified Body Builds Mature Members

In my counseling with married couples, I constantly encounter this misconception that diversity destroys unity.
"We are incompatible. We have irreconcilable differences.
The relationship can no longer work." A moment's reflec-
tion assures such people that their marriage could never
have *begun* unless God had created the differences between
men and women: this unity *requires* diversity!

Consider the various personality types (and their social
backgrounds) which God has raised up and worked into a
single, unified scheme of human redemption: prophets as
nationalistically narrow as Jonah, and as universally compassionate as Isaiah; apostles who had hated Romans (Simon the Zealot), and who had collected taxes for them
(Matthew). Marvel at the diversity of descendants whose
genetic material contributed to the human nature of Jesus
the Messiah.[100] Ponder the potpourri of personalities paraded
past us in the "Hebrew Hall of Faith."[101] If the reader is
weary of my constant variations on the "same old tune,"

---

[99]Eph. 2:19-22. See also Matt. 16:13-19; 21:42-44; 1 Cor. 3:10-17;
1 Peter 2:4-10.
[100]See Matt. 1:1-17; Luke 3:23-38.
[101]See Heb. 11:4ff.

255

please patiently bear with the rest of us who have such difficulty retaining and responding to this truth: *God loves diversity; God is Unity of Being in Diversity of Three Persons; God loves to create unity in (and through) diversity!*

Yet, diversity alone can be threatening and confusing. Without form, diverse elements are a frightening hodgepodge of meaningless molecules. Planets revolving neatly around a central star together constitute a comfortable solar system. Unchained from the sun, those same spheres become only so many floating islands of cold, compressed chaos.

There is reason to be insecure with the thought of simple diversity; however, diversity does not have to lead to chaos. Within the unity of the body of Christ, which has been created by the Spirit of God, we should not fear diversity; we should celebrate it! Because of their very diversity, members of Christ's body must constantly look to the love and grace of God which drew them into the body of Christ.

In turn, contemplation of the love of God in Christ plugs us into an inexhaustible Source of love, binding us together in the one body, and causing us to serve one another with the gifts God has entrusted to us. Holding to Christ, we hold to one another. Thus, we grow together toward the goal of maturity (likeness to Christ, the Head) through every member's ministry of Christ's love:

It was he who gave some to be apostles, some to be proph-
ets, some to be evangelists, and some to be pastors and
teachers, to prepare God's people for works of service, so
***that the body of Christ may be built up** until we all reach*
*unity in the faith and in the knowledge of the Son of God **and***
***become mature,** attaining to the whole measure of the full-*
ness of Christ....we will in all things grow up into him who
is the Head, that is, Christ. From him the whole body, joined
and held together by every supporting ligament, grows and
*builds itself up in love, **as each part does its work.***[102]

Building Up The Body By Lifting Up The Head

Paul, by inspiration of the Spirit of God, consistently sets
forth three key ideas regarding the diversity of gifts which
God has bestowed upon the body of Christ:

1. The source of each member's gifts and abilities
   is the one God who is revealed as Father, Son
   (Christ), and Holy Spirit.

2. Each member of Christ's body is a steward, or
   manager, of the gifts and abilities which God
   entrusts to him or her.

3. The purpose of each member's gifts and abilities
   is the common good of all the members as the
   whole body is built up by the nourishment and
   exercise of love.

---

[102]Eph. 4:11-13, 15-16. Carefully compare Eph. 4:7; Rom. 12:5-
6; 1 Cor. 12:7-11; 14:12, 26.

257

In a healthy human body each cell, each organ, and each member gives itself for the well-being of the whole body. In the healthy Christian community (localized expression of the body of Christ), we are to devote our lives, our property, and our God-given talents and abilities to build up the whole community of which we are members. This is how God wants us to faithfully invest the lives, property, and spiritual gifts He has entrusted to us. Christ's kingdom parables make this clear, and also assure us that in serving the members of the body of Christ, we are serving Christ, the Head.[103]

Each member's gifts and abilities are to be used in *building up* the body of Christ:

> *For even if I boast somewhat freely about the authority the Lord gave us [apostles-L.D.] for building you up rather than pulling you down, I will not be ashamed of it.*[104]

The freedom that comes with a mature comprehension of the gospel of Christ is also a gift of God that is to be exercised in *love,* for *building up* the body of Christ rather than tearing it down:

> *Now about food sacrificed to idols: We know that we all possess knowledge. Knowledge puffs up, but love builds up....We know that an idol is nothing at all in the world and that there is no God but one....But not everyone knows this. Some people are still so accustomed to idols that when they eat such food they think of it as having been sacrificed to an idol....For if anyone with a weak conscience sees you who*

---

[103]Read carefully Matt. 25:14-46.
[104]2 Cor. 10:8. Compare 2 Cor. 13:10.

*have this knowledge eating in an idol's temple, won't he be emboldened to eat what has been sacrificed to idols?...When you sin against your brothers in this way and wound their weak conscience, **you sin against Christ**.*[105]

The proper use of any gift in the body of Christ requires *sensitivity to other members*. The use of any gift to *build up* the body members is a service to Christ, the Head; the abuse of any gift by *tearing down* the body members is a sin against the Head. There is no such thing as loving the invisible God while despising the members of Christ's visible body on earth.[106] It is no use talking about loving the Head while we destroy the body, or of nurturing the Vine as we lop off its branches. Conversely, the solution to the problem of maintaining unity, peace, and love among all the members of the body of Christ is a deliberate devotion to the Head. The members must constantly look to Christ for direction and strength, and lift Him up to one another in their words and deeds. The Corinthian body of believers is a case in point:

I appeal to you, brothers, in the name of our Lord Jesus Christ, that all of you agree with one another so that there may be no divisions among you and that you may be perfectly united in mind and thought. My brothers, some from Chloe's household have informed me that there are quarrels among you. What I mean is this: One of you says, "I follow Paul"; another, "I follow Apollos"; another, "I follow Cephas"; still another, "I follow Christ." Is Christ divided? Was Paul crucified for you? Were you baptized into the name of Paul?...For Christ did not send me to baptize, but to

---

[105]1 Cor. 8:1, 4, 7, 10, 12.   [106]See 1 John 3:1ff; 4:19-21.

259

preach the gospel....For I resolved to know nothing while I was with you except Jesus Christ and him crucified.[107]

Divisions in the body were caused by boasting in human teachers and their "wisdom." Paul immediately responds by reminding the Corinthians of the proclamation of "Christ crucified for sins" which had originally called them into the one body. Their regular celebration of the Lord's Supper was not only a dramatic proclamation of the Lord's death "till He comes," but also a powerful statement of their unity in the body of Christ. Paul reminds them:

Because there is one loaf, we, who are many, are one body, for we all partake of the one loaf.[108]

Wherever we find New Testament Christians failing to hold fast to Christ, the Head, we also find immorality, doctrinal heresy, and selfish ambition threatening the unity and health of the body of Christ:

You foolish Galatians! Who has bewitched you? Before your very eyes Jesus Christ was clearly portrayed as crucified.[109]

Do not let anyone who delights in false humility and the worship of angels disqualify you for the prize. Such a person

---

[107] 1 Cor. 1:10-13, 17; 2:2. Compare 1 Cor. 3:1-4:6ff, in which Paul reminds his Corinthian brothers and sisters that both he and Apollos were servants of Christ for the establishing and building up of God's people. Christ was the foundation on which the Corinthians had been established as God's people, and those who would destroy their unity by divisive teaching incompatible with the gospel would be judged by God.
[108] 1 Cor. 10:17.
[109] Gal. 3:1.

goes into great detail about what he has seen, and his unspiritual mind puffs him up with idle notions. He has lost connection with the Head, from whom the whole body, supported and held together by its ligaments and sinews, grows as God causes it to grow.[110]

See that what you have heard from the beginning remains in you. If it does, you will remain in the Son and in the Father.[111]

The lifting up of Christ draws all kinds of people into the unity of His body.[112] Body members will grow together by using their gifts to serve one another. Attention must be fixed on the Servant, who stripped Himself of heavenly glory so that He could cleanse each member of self-centeredness and make each fit for service in union with the Head. This union with Christ demands visible love:

"A new command I give you: Love one another. As I have loved you, so you must love one another. All men will know that you are my disciples if you love one another."[113]

---

[110]Col. 2:18-19.
[111]1 John 2:24. Compare John 15:1-10.
[112]See John 12:32-33.
[113]John 13:34-35. John's presentation of Jesus as Servant at the so-called Last Supper (John 13:1-17) is a striking dramatic parallel of Paul's Servant Christology (Phil. 2:5-11). Both writers offer strong statements regarding Christ's pre-existent glory as God, both portray the Servant mission in terms of the condescension of Christ, both conclude with an affirmation of Jesus' lordship, and both make ethical application to the Christian community. Compare also John 12:23-26 and 15:1-17, where the themes are surrender of self, union with Christ, and fruitful service.

Each of us, who together form the body of Christ, is *different* from every other member *by God's design.* God's purpose is that our differences might contribute to the building up of a body unified by love. We are all in the process of studying and growing in our comprehension of Christ, the Head. The "one mind" we are to share is Christ's attitude of patient love and humble service toward the members of His body; it is *not* exhaustive agreement on every point of doctrine or life-style. The God who loves diversity designed the Christian community to be a many-celled *body,* not a single-celled amoeba! Truth is a circle (with definite boundaries) within which we stand together; it is not a pin head on which we delicately balance while waiting for each other to fall off.

We are too inclined to issue ultimatums to one another: "Unless you change into what I want you to be within the time I allow, I will have to change my relationship to you." We forget that the body is Christ's, not ours; He is the Head. He alone gives the orders and sets the standards. Missionaries are especially vulnerable to manipulation by those who would try to turn men into puppets by pulling purse strings. Those who claim to be Christ's refuse one another, accuse one another, and abuse one another, just as if Christ had never washed dirty feet; as if He had never bled and died for each member of His spiritual body; as if He had not risen on the third day and ascended to supreme lordship; as if He had never sent the Spirit to unite all of His disciples in one body! The world strains to see some essential difference between itself and those who claim to be Christ's. Are we giving them an excuse for persisting in unbelief, or are we so much like a living body that they can't explain us unless they acknowledge a living Head?[114]

What will stop this incessant bickering among members of Christ's body that causes His name to be "blasphemed among the Gentiles"? What will enable us to receive one another with open arms and with thankful hearts for the God-given gifts that each member brings to the body of Christ?

Consider Paul's exposition of "the most excellent way" to some first century Christians whose self-centeredness, competitiveness, and jealousy of one another has made them perhaps the most talked-about church of the twentieth century:

If I speak in the tongues of men and of angels, but have not love, I am only a resounding gong or a clanging cymbal. If I have the gift of prophecy and can fathom all mysteries and all knowledge, and if I have a faith that can move mountains, but have not love, I am nothing. If I give all I possess to the poor and surrender my body to the flames, but have not love, I gain nothing. Love is patient, love is kind. It does not envy, it does not boast, it is not proud. It is not rude, it is not self-seeking, it is not easily angered, it keeps no record of wrongs. Love does not delight in evil but rejoices with the truth. It always protects, always trusts, always hopes, always perseveres. Love never fails.[115]

---

[114]Read carefully John 13:34-45; 17:20-23.
[115]1 Cor. 13:1-8.

Divisions in the body of Christ are not always geographically or physically manifested: Christians with deep-seated animosities toward one another can continue to meet together (even *live* together) under one roof for years. The Corinthian manifestation of division had nothing to do with geography; it had everything to do with a lack of love. It was ugly then, and it is still ugly among modern Christians. And it will continue to mar the message we hold forth until you and I stand up boldly, in righteous indignation (*not* in self-righteous pride), and say clearly: "Enough!"

Brothers and sisters in Christ, let us stop promoting ourselves, and begin to lift up Christ. Let us receive one another, minister to one another, and enjoy one another, as Christ has received each one of us. Let us use our gifts to build up one another in love as members of the one body of which Christ alone is Head.

15

EVERY MEMBER A MINISTER!

Jesus warned His disciples against a careless attitude about "words." Modern man's attitude regarding words has tended toward the same lack of depth, clarity, and definition that marks the rest of his life. Not believing in any final, absolute authority in the universe, every person has become a "god" unto himself or herself.

This same attitude of anarchy that tossed aside the authority of Scripture has declared its independence of the dictionary, as well. Words no longer have any solid, objective meaning outside the heads of those who speak and hear. Conversation can be prolonged for hours without any real communication of content. Such a mentality poses an awesome challenge to those who seek to teach and live under the authority of God's revealed Word. We must insist on clear definitions and agreement in terminology.

Words must be given their biblical meanings, and not just whatever meaning seems to fit the situation, or the speaker's personal preference. We have already looked at some of the problems caused by the careless, superficial usage of the word "church." Over a relatively short span of time, the original biblical ideas behind this word have been almost completely undermined in popular thinking.

In even the most casual contexts, words are powerful tools that convey and reinforce the ideas that shape a society. What we say is often not what we really mean. However, if we continually say things we don't really mean, we may one day forget what we originally meant; we may begin to mean something entirely different.

Grace And Faith

It is obvious that Christians must understand the biblical meaning of the words "grace" and "faith" if they are to hold to the gospel firmly, and communicate it clearly to those outside the Christian community. But the words "grace" and "faith" are also vitally related to our understanding of what it means to participate in the body of Christ. After urging the Christians of Rome to respond to God's mercies by offering their bodies and minds to God, the apostle Paul wrote:

266

*For by the **grace given** me I say to every one of you: Do not think of yourself more highly than you ought, but rather think of yourself with sober judgment, in accordance with the measure of **faith God has given** you. Just as each of us has one body with many members, and these members do not all have the same function, so in Christ we who are many form one body, and each member belongs to all the others. We have different **gifts**, according to the **grace given** us. If a man's **gift** is prophesying, let him **use it in proportion to his faith**. If it is serving, let him serve; if it is teaching, let him teach....*[116]*

From this and other related passages, it is clear that the general biblical ideas behind "grace" and "faith" hold true in their application to spiritual gifts in the body of Christ: "Grace" is God's generous bestowal of gifts and undeserved blessings; "faith" is man's capacity to receive and exercise what God entrusts to his stewardship.

Throughout Scripture, grace and faith are complimentary concepts; the gracious intention of God will not be fulfilled without a corresponding response of faith from man. But what can easily escape our awareness is that God not only gives the grace; He also gives the faith by which man exercises the grace! He gives the gift, and the capacity to *use* the gift. Read it again: "in accordance with the measure of faith God has given you." In the whole process of salvation, God initiates and man responds. It is God who creates each individual in His own image, with free will to trust and act (believe and behave); it is God who purposed, prophesied, and finally presented redemption in Christ to

---

[116]Rom. 12:3-7. Compare Rom.1:5; Eph. 3:2, 7-9; 1 Peter 4:10-11.

fallen humanity "in the fullness of the time"; it is God who confronts each accountable human being in the proclamation of the gospel of Christ. It is God who providentially prepares, calls, and incorporates each member of Christ's body, and who equips each part to play a unique role in the Christian community.[117] Salvation in Christ is *entirely* "by grace through faith":

> *It is because of him that you are in Christ Jesus, who has become for us wisdom from God—that is, our righteousness, holiness and redemption.*[118]

Gifts, Ministries, Workings

Another biblical word that has suffered much misunderstanding and abuse in our relativistic, secularized culture is "minister." Certain religious communities that rightly place a high value on the biblical concept of "priesthood of all believers" have long objected to other communities which recognize a specialized clergy. While I sympathize with their objection against creating a class system among the members of Christ's body, it seems inconsistent to find fault with an exclusivist *priesthood* system while supporting an exclusivist *minister* system. "This is John Smith, the minister." Our language says more than we intend to convey. But if we do not intend to say that John Smith, as *the* minister, is in some sense a more vital and important member of the body than any other, why do we speak thus? If we don't really desire to imply that the one who publicly proclaims the gospel or exhorts the congregation has a ministry in the body that is qualitatively superior to any

---

[117] See Rom. 8:28-30; 2 Thess. 2:13-15; 1 Cor. 1:4-9.
[118] 1 Cor. 1:30.

other, we should choose our words more carefully. And if we find nothing objectionable in describing those who labor in the Word of God as "ministers" in an exclusive, prominent sense, then we should cease to find fault with those who claim to be "priests" in a hierarchical sense! Above all, let us refuse to divide the body of Christ over words that are not clearly defined and related to the truth of the gospel.

It is the thesis of this book that every single member of the body of Christ is a minister. For those who may be thinking that I am speaking only figuratively, technically, analogically, or in any other sense than literally, I must immediately clarify my position: *God has given every member of the Christian community special gifts, and appointed each one a special place in the structure of the community in which to express that ministry for the building up of the whole body of Christ.*

> *There are different kinds of gifts [**charismata**], but the same Spirit. There are different kinds of service [**diakonia**, the usual New Testament word for **ministries**-L.D.], but the same Lord. There are different kinds of working [**energema**], but the same God works all of them in all men.*[119]

---

[119]1 Cor. 12:4-6. See also 1 Cor. 12:7-11, 27-28; Eph. 4:7-11; James 1:17. "Unity in diversity" is clearly the key to understanding both the nature of the body of Christ and the nature of the Godhead from whom all the ministers and ministries originate. The same "Spirit," the one "Lord" (Christ), and the only "God" (Father) are equally attributed with equipping the members of the body and appointing them their ministries. Paul's theme in the "body" passages is *"different"* (manifestations of grace to the body), but *"the same"* (divine Source behind all of them).

269

Each member of the Christian community has a gift from God which is to be applied for the benefit of the whole body of Christ. The ministry which God appoints for each member in the body is in accordance with the measure of faith He has supplied to each member. One's capacity for ministry is in proportion to his or her capacity to receive and invest the gracious gifts of God. God entrusts different gifts to different members, and appoints different ministries to each one. That is why it is foolish and wrong to envy the ministry of another, or to force the ministry of other members into the mold of one's own. God grant each of us both the honesty and the humility of Paul, who could rejoice in his own gifts while glorifying God for the gifts of others:

> *I wish that all men were as I am. But each man has his own gift from God; one has this gift, another has that.*[120]

Church As Body And Bride

In a wonderful passage, Paul weaves together the relationships of Christ to church, head to body, and husband to wife in such a tight, close-knit pattern that the three strands are hardly distinguishable:

> *Wives, submit to your husbands as to the Lord. For the husband is the head of the wife as Christ is the head of the church, his body, of which he is the Savior. Now as the church submits to Christ, so also wives should submit to their husbands in everything. Husbands, love your wives, just as Christ loved the church and gave himself up for her to make her holy, cleansing her by the washing with water*

---

[120]1 Cor. 7:7.

270

through the word, and to present her to himself as a radiant church, without stain or wrinkle or any other blemish, but holy and blameless. In this same way, husbands ought to love their wives as their own bodies. He who loves his wife loves himself. After all, no one ever hated his own body, but he feeds and cares for it, just as Christ does the church—for we are members of his body. "For this reason a man will leave his father and mother and be united to his wife, and the two will become one flesh." This is a profound mystery—but I am talking about Christ and the church. However, each one of you also must love his wife as he loves himself, and the wife must respect her husband.[121]

As head and body are "one flesh" (a unit—like bow and arrow, lock and key, violin and bow), so also are husband and wife. But both of these natural relationships are analogies that illustrate a higher relationship, which is revealed by the Spirit through Paul: the relationship of Christ to His church. The authority of the husband over the wife is to be modeled after the pattern of Christ's authority over the church. The submission of the wife to the husband is likened to the church's submission to Christ. The husband's love, care, and self-sacrifice on behalf of his wife should reflect Christ's redeeming self-sacrifice and continuing care for His church.

In marriage, the husband and wife are no longer merely separate, independent units; they have merged together to form another, higher kind of complimentary "oneness," in which each belongs to the other:

[121]Eph. 5:22-33. Compare 2 Cor. 11:2-4; John 3:29-30; Rev. 19:9; 21:2-3, 9-14.

> *The wife's body does not belong to her alone but also to her husband. In the same way, the husband's body does not belong to him alone but also to his wife.*[122]

In Christ, members of the body belong to the Head, and the church collectively belongs to Christ, by right of purchase (redemption):

> *Do you not know that your bodies are members of Christ himself?...Do you not know that he who unites himself with a prostitute is one with her in body? For it is said, "The two will become one flesh." But he who unites himself with the Lord is one with him in spirit....Do you not know that your body is a temple of the Holy Spirit, who is in you, whom you have received from God? You are not your own; you were bought at a price. Therefore honor God with your body.*[123]

Because we belong to Christ as members of His one body, we belong to one another. The Head assigns each of us to minister His gifts to one another. In the Christian community, in the body of Christ, what I have is yours and what you have is mine. Yet, we are not to make disrespectful, presumptuous demands upon one another's stewardships; rather, there are to be relationships of spontaneous, practical love and living sacrifice among the members, motivated by the love of God revealed in Christ:

> *Therefore, I urge you, brothers, in view of God's mercy, to offer your bodies as living sacrifices....Just as each of us has one body with many members, and these members do not all have the same function, so in Christ we who are many form one body, and each member belongs to all the others.*[124]

---

[122] 1 Cor. 7:4.
[123] 1 Cor. 6:15-17, 19-20. See also Acts 20:28; 1 Peter 1:19-20; Eph. 1:7.
[124] Rom. 12:1, 4-5.

In Christ, we neither take advantage of one another, nor hold one another at arm's length. The proper attitude is mutual submission, not mutual suspicion.

Carry each other's burdens, and in this way you will fulfill the law of Christ.[125]

God may not have entrusted your gift to me, but your gift becomes mine in the setting of the one body in which we both share. Envy, competition, and pride are totally out of place in the body of Christ:

So then, no more boasting about men! All things are yours, whether Paul or Apollos or Cephas or the world or life or death or the present or the future—all are yours, and you are of Christ, and Christ is of God.[126]

Principles And Practical Application

The body is a unit, though it is made up of many parts; and though all its parts are many, they form one body. So it is with Christ. For we were all baptized by the one Spirit into the one body—whether Jews or Greeks, slave or free—and we were all given the one Spirit to drink. Now the body is not made up of one part but of many....If they were all one part, where would the body be? As it is, there are many parts, but one body....If one part suffers, every part suffers with it; if one part is honored, every part rejoices with it. Now you are the body of Christ, and each one of you is a part of it.[127]

Our significance in God's purpose is not in our isolated capacities, but in our *body membership:* our contribution

---

[125]Gal. 6:2. Compare Matt. 24:45-51; Luke 12:35-48.
[126]1 Cor. 3:21-22.
[127]1 Cor. 12:12-14, 19-20, 26-27.

as members of the one body. Consider the following principles and their practical applications:

1. *All gifts are given by the grace of the one God.*

2. *Not all minister-members have the same gifts; no two have identical expression.*[128]

3. *Each steward-minister is entrusted with talents "according to his (or her) ability."*[129] A failure to understand this principle will lead to frustration, confusion, and an identity crisis concerning one's personal significance in the body of Christ. Our lives change, and our ministries must adapt accordingly. Things we once could not do, we now can do; things we did when we were younger, we no longer can do. One's ministry may change, but it does not end as long as membership in the body is a reality.

4. *There is no biblical distinction between "secular" and "sacred" gifts.*[130] I have a brother in Christ who is a skilled wood craftsman, and he has offered that gift to God as a ministry in the body of Christ. He and I have ministered to one another and to others of the local Christian community: he in making furniture, and I in teaching the Word of God. The two ministries are from the one God; neither is less sacred or

---

[128]See Rom. 12:6-8; 1 Cor. 12:4-11.
[129]See Matt. 25:14-15; 1 Cor. 7:7.
[130]Read carefully Exod. 31:3,6; Judg. 14:6; 3:10. Compare 1 Peter 4:10-11.

more secular than the other. The Bible does not even exalt supernatural manifestations of God's grace above natural abilities; both are God-given, to serve the one body.[131] In Christ, one's whole "secular" life becomes sanctified, set apart for God's purpose in building up the body of Christ. Some things once done for selfish motives are now done to glorify God; natural talents become sacred gifts when they are offered to the Head through ministry to His body. Do you fix cars? Fix them for Jesus. Do you clean buildings or paint houses? Whatever you do for your brothers and sisters in the body is done for Christ. Every member is a minister.

5. *God calls each member to use every gracious gift of talent, skill, ability, and ministry which He has bestowed for His redemptive purposes in building up the body of Christ.* We are responsible as stewards of the grace of God; we can choose to answer His call by faithfully ministering His grace according to the capacities, abilities, and opportunities He entrusts to us. Or, we can refuse to invest what He has entrusted to us, and bury it in excuses instead.[132] Self-centeredness will reveal itself in laziness and irresponsibility; love will motivate us to fulfill our ministries for the building up of the body of Christ.

---

[131]See 1 Cor. 12:28; Rom. 12:6-8; Eph. 4:11; 1 Peter 4:10-11.
[132]Read carefully Matt. 25:14-46; 2 Cor. 8:12.

*From him the whole body, joined and held to-
gether by every supporting ligament, grows and
builds itself up in love, as each part does its
work.*[133]

6. *Every member, as a minister, is an individual
   expression of the coordinated body of Christ.*
   Each member is coordinated, integrated, and or-
   chestrated with all the other members by relationship to the one Head, Jesus Christ. Since
   each member has submitted in obedient faith to
   the same saving truth (the gospel of Christ), each
   is in covenant relationship, not only with God,
   but also with the other body members. Every
   member finds proper relationship to the whole
   body by looking primarily to the Head—not to
   oneself or one's fellow-members:

*I care very little if I am judged by you or by any
human court; indeed, I do not even judge myself.
My conscience is clear, but that does not make me
innocent. It is the Lord who judges me.*[134]

*We do not dare to classify or compare ourselves
with some who commend themselves. When they
measure themselves by themselves and compare
themselves with themselves they are not wise....
But, "Let him who boasts boast in the Lord."
For it is not the one who commends himself who is
approved, but the one whom the Lord commends.*[135]

---

[133]Eph. 4:16.
[134]1 Cor. 4:3-4.
[135]2 Cor. 10:12, 17-18.

276

7. *No member's gift is more important than other members' gifts, nor is any member more important than any other member.* I am aware that certain gifts are closely associated with ministries that are foundational in the structure of the church, while others are not.[136] For example, apostles and prophets are said to hold foundational positions in the church which have certainly served the body of Christ in a greater capacity than other positions. But two things must be said. First, the ministry of a body member is not identical with his or her "gifts"; the ministry is the *stewardship* of that which God has entrusted to him or her. Paul wrote concerning his position of apostleship:

> *Surely you have heard about* **the administration** *of God's grace that was given to me for you....I became a servant of this gospel by the gift of God's grace given me through the working of his power.*[137]

One *ministry* may be more productive or spectacular than another; one's *capacity* to receive and administer God's grace may be greater or less than another's. But one's *gift* or participation is no more important than another member's:

---

[136]See Eph. 2:20; 4:11f and compare 1 Cor. 12:28.
[137]Eph. 3:2, 7.

> From him the whole body, joined and held to-
> gether by *every supporting ligament*, grows and
> builds itself up in love, *as each part does its
> work.*[138]

Second, each member is gifted, but none is self-
sufficient. The grace of God is expressed in every ministry; there is no place for egotism, pride,
or condemnation of another's ministry. We are
not to "rate" one another.

> *For who makes you different from anyone else?
> What do you have that you did not receive? And if
> you did receive it, why do you boast as though you
> did not?*[139]

8. *Each member's gifts and ministry contribute to
   the common good of the whole body.* The body,
   as a whole, is incomplete without every
   member's ministry. Gifts are to be "pursued"
   (exercised; developed; eagerly desired) for the
   sake of ministry to other body members, that the
   whole body may be edified (built up in faith,
   hope, and love):

> *Until I come, devote yourself to the public read-
> ing of Scripture, to preaching and to teaching.
> Do not neglect your gift, which was given you
> through a prophetic message when the body of
> elders laid their hands on you. Be diligent in
> these matters; give yourself wholly to them, so
> that everyone may see your progress. Watch
> your life and doctrine closely. Persevere in*

---

[138]Eph. 4:16.
[139]1 Cor. 4:7.

them, because if you do, you will save both your-
self and your hearers.[140]

*For this reason I remind you to fan into flame
the gift of God, which is in you through the lay-
ing on of my hands. For God did not give us a
spirit of timidity, but a spirit of power, of love
and of self-discipline.*[141]

*Since you are eager to have spiritual gifts, try to
excel in gifts that build up the church.*[142]

9. *The essential application of the biblical teaching
regarding gifts and ministry in the body of Christ
is that the unique identity and abilities of each
member should be expressed in loving, serving
relationships.*

This implies the necessity of unity and harmony
among the members of the Christian community,
as well as regular interaction and involvement
with one another's lives. Moral purity and a central emphasis on the clear, pure gospel of Christ
are also indispensable for self-expression in a
context of unity, love, and mutual service.

---

[140] 1 Tim. 4:13-16.

[141] 2 Tim. 1:6-7.

[142] 1 Cor. 14:12. Compare 1 Cor. 12:31; 14:1. My reference to the
Corinthian passages is not intended to address modern claims concerning supernatural manifestations of the Spirit, but merely to
emphasize the principle that the most desirable gifts are those that
most build up the body.

Affirmation of each individual member as a minister to the Christian community means that the creative application of the gifts of each member finds expression and acceptance in the body. There are many opportunities and possibilities in daily life for Christians to serve, encourage, teach, edify, and comfort one another. However, members cannot be a part *of* one another if they are always apart *from* one another. Geographical distance is hard to overcome, but prayer and modern technology can span the miles. Far worse, and harder to overcome, is the distance between people that results from indifference and cold self-centeredness. Members of the body of Christ should cultivate pure, close, loving relationships with one another.

10. *Members of the body of Christ belong to one another and minister with their individual gifts according to each one's measure of faith, to the building up of the entire body.* An anonymous article from a church bulletin which recently crossed my desk offered the following observation:

> In the church today, we have come to think of only one man in the congregation as being the minister. The ministry is not something done to the church, but something done by the church.

This Christian brother was addressing an imbalance in the popular perception of "ministry"; it *is* an "every member" affair, and not just a one-man show. But I would caution against the opposite extreme; ministry is practiced in the context of the body. Ministry *is* done "to the church," as well as *by* the church. Every member is a minister in relation to the whole community, serving other members and thus contributing to the growth of the whole body. In an age in which "bigger" is popularly equated with "better," God's people would do well to seriously ponder the prophet's question:

"Who despises the day of small things?" [143]

Each of us has something to give; let us not minimize the importance of that "something," whatever it may be. A humble staff in the hand of Moses, a few loaves and a couple of dried fish in the hands of a small boy: if God can accomplish so much with so little, what could he do with you and me, if we truly put ourselves completely in His hands? To concern ourselves about the size of our ministry is to be distracted from faithfulness to our charge. Our responsibility is to minister the grace of God, and let God produce the fruit. The unsigned article I referred to previously went on to note, concerning the church:

Too many of the sons of God come to be ministered unto, rather than to minister.

___

[143]Zech. 4:10.

The result is that the saints are no longer participants in the arena, but spectators in the grandstand. Somewhere along the way we have missed the very essence of the Christian concept, and the result is that we have the greatest accumulation of unused talent and the richest deposit of untouched ability of any group of people on the earth.

Can we be complacent about this unbiblical state of affairs in view of Christ's clear and solemn admonition to each of us?

> *"Be on guard! Be alert! You do not know when that time will come. It's like a man going away: He leaves his house in charge of his servants, each with his assigned task, and tells the one at the door to keep watch. Therefore keep watch because you do not know when the owner of the house will come back—whether in the evening, or at midnight, or when the rooster crows, or at dawn. If he comes suddenly, do not let him find you sleeping. What I say to you, I say to everyone: 'Watch!'"* [144]

May we allow God to draw us together as members of Christ's body, and to use the talents that He has graciously entrusted to each of us for His glory in the building up of one another.

---

[144]Mark 13:33-37.

16

EVERY MEMBER'S
SUPREME GIFT

I long to see you so that I may impart to you some spiritual gift to make you strong—that is, that you and I may be mutually encouraged by each other's faith.[145]

This final chapter will be devoted to a serious consideration of the one supreme gift which God has bequeathed to each of His children in Christ. Without this gift, no other gift will function in proper ministry within the body of Christ. No part of the body can do its work as God intended unless it is using this supreme gift in its ministry. I am speaking of our legacy of divine love.

It is no coincidence that in every major New Testament text regarding spiritual gifts, the love of God in Christ is

---

[145]Rom. 1:11-12.

discussed in close proximity. Love is the key that unlocks every other gift for building up the body into the likeness of Christ, the Head:

We have different gifts, according to the grace given us....Love must be sincere. Hate what is evil; cling to what is good. Be devoted to one another in brotherly love. Honor one another above yourselves. Never be lacking in zeal, but keep your spiritual fervor, serving the Lord. Be joyful in hope, patient in affliction, faithful in prayer. Share with God's people who are in need. Practice hospitality.[146]

Are all apostles? Are all prophets? Are all teachers? Do all work miracles? Do all have gifts of healing? Do all speak in tongues? Do all interpret? But eagerly desire the greater gifts. And now I will show you the most excellent way. If I speak in the tongues of men and of angels, but have not love, I am only a resounding gong or a clanging symbol. If I have the gift of prophecy and can fathom all mysteries and all knowledge, and if I have a faith that can move mountains, but have not love, I am nothing.[147]

It was he who gave some to be apostles, some to be prophets, some to be evangelists, and some to be pastors and teachers, to prepare God's people for works of service, so that the body of Christ may be built up....Then we will no longer be infants, tossed back and forth by the waves, and blown here and there by every wind of teaching and by the cunning and craftiness of men in their deceitful scheming. Instead, speaking the truth in love, we will in all things grow up into him who is the Head, that is, Christ. From him the whole body, joined and held together by every supporting ligament, grows and builds itself up in love, as each part does its work.[148]

---

[146]Rom. 12:6, 9-13.   [147]1 Cor. 12:29-13:2.
[148]Eph. 4:11-12, 14-16.

Above all, love each other deeply, because love covers over a multitude of sins. Offer hospitality to one another without grumbling. Each one should use whatever gift he has received to serve others, faithfully administering God's grace in its various forms.[149]

Love Is Personal

I have already emphasized the nature of the Christian community as a living organism (body) rather than an institution. The body of Christ should prayerfully seek godly wisdom to find forms of expression that will not hinder the spiritual life which animates it, but will instead nourish and promote that life. Institutional structure can easily become so powerful and overwhelming that the personal aspect of the living body of Christ is lost.

The body of Christ is made up of people with personal problems and needs that really have nothing to do with high-powered organization or brick and mortar. There is a danger that life in the Christian community can become so "loose" that it degenerates into disorder and chaos, as reflected in Paul's First Epistle to the Corinthians.[150] But we should remember that orderliness and structure are supposed to *serve* the life of the body, not stifle it.

It is easy to mistake the external, incidental "trappings" of a relationship for the reality of the relationship itself. A husband and a wife may spend years under the same roof, accumulating possessions, paying off the home mortgage,

---

[149]1 Peter 4:8-10.
[150]See especially 1 Cor. 14:26-40.

providing for their children, achieving "respectability" as a fine, solid family according to the standards of their community. But what happens if all of these trappings of solid family life have only masked the lack of real family relationships? Our generation is living proof of the tragic results: children turn away from values their parents preached but never practiced; husbands and wives discover that they have little in common and nothing to say to each other, now that the kids have left home.

The same sad story can be told of many expressions of Christian community: all the "trappings" are in place, but in the end they become only a "trap," a snare. Our meetings and programs and functions can deceive us into believing that we are still building on a solid foundation which we really abandoned long ago. A lack of reality in present relationships cannot be justified by a devotion that may have existed in the past, and the trophies that we offer as evidence of our fidelity may turn and mock us with accusations of spiritual adultery:

> *"Not everyone who says to me, 'Lord, Lord,' will enter the kingdom of heaven, but only he who does the will of my Father who is in heaven. Many will say to me on that day, 'Lord, Lord, did we not prophesy in your name, and in your name drive out demons and perform many miracles?' Then I will tell them plainly, 'I never knew you. Away from me, you evildoers!'"* [151]

---

[151]Matt. 7:21-23. Jesus had just warned His disciples that false teachers ("wolves," "bad trees") could be known by their "fruits." Obviously, prophesying, exorcising demons, and working miracles are not decisive criteria in determining genuine discipleship. See also Rev. 2-3.

The reality of person-to-person relationships in the Christian community is not a negotiable item; it cannot be compromised or sold out in the interests of ecclesiastical institutionalism. The body of Christ is the family of God, and personal relationships are indispensable to healthy family life.

Love is the stuff of which strong personal relationships are made. It can be embodied in many forms, but no contrived program can substitute for the real thing. Love refuses to be confined by a schedule; it is on call twenty-four hours a day, as personal human needs arise. It does not punch a time clock, nor is it "off duty" when the final "amen" signals the beginning of the human stampede toward the parking lot of the saints.

Love Is Mutual

Some gifts in the body of Christ are highly individual stewardships; not everyone has them. Not every ministry can be "mutual," nor should this be the case. If you offer me exactly the same ministries that I offer you, the question would arise as to whether we really need each other. But there is one ministry, one gift, that each member has been given and which each member needs to share with others in the body: the gift of love. Besides encompassing our specialized personal ministries, the ministry of love also manifests itself in certain "one another" capacities that I have listed in an appendix to this book. We owe one another these various manifestations of the ministry of love:

*Let no debt remain outstanding, except the continuing debt
to love one another, for he who loves his fellow man has fulfilled the law.*[152]

Mutual ministries are reciprocal; they work on a "two-way
street." These "one another" ministries are giving-and-re-
ceiving relationships in which each member of the body is
called to share.

Love's Basic Attitude: Humility

God's love is the underlying reality that must exist among
members of the Christian community in order for there to
be healthy relationships of mutual ministry. The Spirit of
God pours out divine love into each Christian's heart
when he or she responds in obedient faith to the truth of
the gospel of Christ.

*...God has poured out his love into our hearts by the Holy
Spirit, whom he has given us.*[153]

*Now that you have purified yourselves by obeying the truth
so that you have sincere love for your brothers, love one another deeply....*[154]

---

[152]Rom. 13:8. Compare Rom. 1:14-15; 8:3-4; 2 Cor. 5:14-21; Gal.
5:13-18; Matt. 22:34-40; James 2:8-13. God's love revealed in the
gospel of Christ causes us to understand that we owe love to all
whom God has loved in Christ. In so loving others, we fulfill the
intent of all God's commandments. We "fulfill righteousness" by
loving God and neighbor, as the gospel teaches and the indwelling
Spirit enables.
[153]Rom. 5:5. Paul goes on to remind his readers of the love of God
in Christ revealed in the gospel message (Rom. 5:6-8).
[154]1 Peter 1:22. Peter identifies "the truth" which his readers had
obeyed: "the word that was preached to you" (1 Peter 1:23-25).

Through the gospel message, the Holy Spirit purifies the Christian's heart so that sincere (non-hypocritical) love can be expressed toward other Christians, and toward all people. This approach to right relationships, based on a personal relationship with a gracious God from whom all true holiness and love flow, is completely opposite to the legalistic approach to righteousness. Legalists tend to make right relationships primarily a matter of abstract rule-keeping, completely divorced from an understanding of God's holy and loving character. They seem to regard God as a shyster lawyer who can be favorably impressed with clever legal loopholes and technical maneuvers. Theirs is an impersonal, external emphasis which effectively shuts the true Person of God out of their lives, and inevitably leads to dichotomy and hypocrisy: the "religion of man" versus the "righteousness of God." The legalistic approach also produces a harvest of self-righteous pride, contemptuous criticism, petty jealousies, and other ego-centric attitudes that make real human relationships most difficult.

In contrast to this ugly lack of reality and personal integrity, the basis of Christ's approach to relationships with God and man is love. His love within us is the fruit of His Spirit, who dwells in us as we trust God's revelation of love and mercy in the gospel of Christ. This love brings forth a healthy humility and reverence toward God, one-self, and all human "selves" created in God's image, for whom Christ died. It promotes mutual acceptance and service among members of the body of Christ. This humility sets us free to rejoice in God's grace, and to confess our sins to God and to other members of the body who can minister to us and pray for us. The need for pride and pretense is gone. Members of Christ's body are set free to serve one another from a motivation of pure divine love.

Think about it: Isn't it really self-centeredness, rising up in the form of pride, which keeps us from submitting to Christ (the Head) by faithfully serving our brothers and sisters in His body? Why is the thought of washing one another's feet so unthinkable to us, when the One whom we call "Lord" washed dirty feet as an example for us?

> *Therefore, rid yourselves of all malice and all deceit, hypocrisy, envy, and slander of every kind.*[155]

> *Therefore, I urge you, brothers, in view of God's mercy, to offer your bodies as living sacrifices, holy and pleasing to God—which is your spiritual worship....For by the grace given me I say to every one of you: Do not think of yourself more highly than you ought, but rather think of yourself with sober judgment....Love must be sincere.*[156]

In the body of Christ, we are motivated by God's love to offer ourselves to God and to one another. All of our gifts are sanctified (made holy) by the supernatural love of God, as we offer them in worship to God by serving one another. The love of God in our hearts makes the difference as to whether one's ministry is being done in the flesh or in the Spirit. A spiritual ministry has certain identifying characteristics.

---

[155]1 Peter 2:1.
[156]Rom. 12:1, 3, 9.

Is God Being Glorified?

Jesus' historical ministry was characterized by a persistent refusal to glorify Himself; He pointed men toward the Father, who spoke and worked through Him.[157] The pattern of Jesus glorifying the Father gives us a way to determine whether our own gifts and ministries are glorifying God. Whatever our ministry might be, are we doing it primarily for selfish reasons? Is it a self-seeking enterprise? Don't be misled into believing that you cannot be paid by human beings if you want to offer a ministry to God. "The workman is worthy of his hire." Jesus and His apostles received support from those to whom they ministered.

The issue is one of motivation: Is this paycheck (or compensation) dedicated to God's will, or my own? Have I dedicated my work to the God who enables me to earn my living, or am I self-deceived in believing that *I* am the source of my skills? And don't think for a moment that driving a taxi cannot bring glory to God. Any lawful employment or service can glorify God when offered to Him in humble thanks and praise.

Does It Build Up The Body?

Whatever ministry advances God's eternal purpose in Christ brings glory to God:

---

[157]For example, see John 5:19-23, 41-44; 7:16-18; 8:28-29, 49-50, 54; 10:26, 37-38; 12:44-45, 49-50; 13:31-32; 14:10-11, 24, 31; 17:4-5. Contrast the attitude of the Pharisees described in Matt. 6:1-18; Luke 18:9-14.

*Now to him who is able to do immeasurably more than all we ask or imagine, according to his power that is at work within us, **to him be glory in the church and in Christ Jesus throughout all generations,** forever and ever! Amen.*[158]

God's purpose in Christ involves both Head (Jesus) and body (the church). The Head and body are so intimately related in the purpose of God that to sin against the church is to sin against Christ; to serve the church is to serve Christ.[159] Is my ministry related in some way to strengthening, nourishing, or reviving the people of God? A spiritual ministry builds up the body of Christ. It is no less "spiritual" to serve the physical needs of members than to serve the non-physical needs. Man doesn't live on bread alone, but neither can he survive in this world without physical sustenance.

In those days when the number of disciples was increasing, the Grecian Jews among them complained against those of the Aramaic-speaking community because their widows were being overlooked in the daily distribution of food. So the Twelve gathered all the disciples together and said, "It would not be right for us to neglect the ministry of the word of God in order to wait on tables. Brothers, choose seven men from among you who are known to be full of the Spirit and wisdom. We will turn this responsibility over to them and will give our attention to prayer and the ministry of the word."[160]

The Twelve had received a ministry from Christ. The Seven were given a different ministry, but it was no less spiritual than the ministry of prayer and teaching. In fact,

---

[158]Eph. 3:20-21.
[159]Recall Acts 9:1-5; 22:1-8; 26:9-15; Col. 1:24.
[160]Acts 6:1-4.

these Seven, in whose ministry most New Testament scholars find the basis of the deacon's work, had to meet high spiritual qualifications.[161] Let us avoid the mistake of making an absolute dichotomy between the spiritual and the material. As someone has noted: "God likes matter. He created a lot of it, and called it 'good.'" In Christ, mammon can be devoted to God. That which God originally made "very good" has often been forced to serve evil purposes. In Christ, it may again become holy.

Is It Edifying?

There may be some way to build up the body of Christ without building up its individual members in the process, but I cannot conceive of it. One's ministry will glorify God as it builds up the body of Christ by edifying its members. "Edification" is a broad term with many possible applications, but it must certainly include sensitivity toward the needs of the spiritually weak,[162] as well as practical care for the needs of the total person who is in Christ.[163] Does your ministry in some way contribute to building up Christians by meeting their personal and material needs?

Is It Enjoyable?

Whether or not we "have fun" while serving Jesus and one another is not the point here. The question is, do you find

---

[161]See 1 Tim. 3:8-13 regarding deacon's qualifications.
[162]See 1 Cor. 8:1-13; 10:31-11:1; 2 Cor. 11:29; Rom. 15:1-3; Gal. 6:1-2.
[163]Read Matt. 25:31-46 and compare James 2:14-17; 1 John 3:16-18; Heb. 13:1-3.

joy in your particular ministry? Joy is second only to love in Paul's description of the fruit of the Spirit. Jesus said, "Deny yourself," not "Enjoy yourself." However, there is great joy in following Jesus Christ, in doing the will of God, in knowing that God is present and is pleased with your service. There may be situations in which the task God sets before us is not enjoyable. Then we, like our Forerunner Jesus, will have to look beyond the immediate circumstances, to the joy set before us.[164] This is usually the exception rather than the rule, however. The "abundant life" that Jesus brings to us is not a constant stress test, nor did Jesus Himself agonize nightly as in Gethsemene. There are seasons of trial and seasons of refreshing, but through it all should flow a joy of deep-seated fulfillment and contentment. Salvation means (among other things) being *found:* coming to know and understand and accept ourselves, as God knows and understands and accepts us in Christ.

> But Zacchaeus stood up and said to the Lord, "Look, Lord! Here and now I give half of my possessions to the poor, and if I have cheated anybody out of anything, I will pay back four times the amount." Jesus said to him, "Today salvation has come to this house, because this man, too, is a son of Abraham. For the Son of Man came to seek and to save what was lost."[165]

Sometimes it happens that people escape from being squeezed into the mold of the world, only to find themselves being squeezed into the mold of a narrow-minded

---

[164]See Heb. 12:2.   [165]Luke 19:8-10.

Christian community. They are not allowed to "find themselves" in the body of Christ; they are subjected to the "Christian cookie cutter," which cuts away everything about them that doesn't resemble every other member of the church. Think how much human personality is wasted in this process: all that precious "cookie dough" that God made, that Christ died for—thrown away! In contrast, consider what the Spirit says to the churches through Paul, the apostle:

> *We have different gifts, according to the grace given us. If a man's gift is prophesying, **let him use it** in proportion to his faith. If it is serving, **let him serve**; if it is teaching, **let him teach**; if it is encouraging, **let him encourage**; if it is contributing to the needs of others, **let him give generously**; if it is leadership, **let him govern diligently**; if it is showing mercy, **let him do it cheerfully**.*[166]

Each minister-member must have freedom to give himself to his own unique ministry. In many cases, there have been those within the Christian community (often leaders) who have tried to put pressure on fellow members to stop doing some good work of faith in order to pursue some other ministry. "You ought to be doing this instead of that," say these self-appointed "talent scouts for Christ."

It is one thing to encourage a Christian brother or sister to consider possible areas of personal ministry that have never been explored; it is entirely another thing to set oneself up as the judge of what ministry that brother or sister "ought (or ought not) to be doing."

---

[166]Rom. 12:6-8.

Mary of Bethany was criticized for *her* ministry. But Jesus responded to her critics with these words:

"Leave her alone....Why are you bothering her?" [167]

Brothers and sisters in Christ, let us obey our Lord in this matter! We must stop "bothering" each other regarding our service and ministries. Instead, let us bless and encourage one another. The next time you see a brother or sister being criticized for their loving service, say to the critic: "Leave her (him) alone....Why are you bothering her (him)?"

Ministry Or Misery?

Ministry in the body of Christ should be a joy motivated by love, not a drudgery motivated by guilt. There is a strange misconception among many Christians that God's will for them cannot possibly coincide with their own happiness. "If I like this, it must be wrong. God doesn't want His people to enjoy their lives in this world." What a misunderstanding of God's character this thinking reveals! Consider the alternative to a ministry of joy: Does God desire that His people go through life in this world with clenched teeth, rigid jaw muscles, furrowed brows, and excess stomach acid? Is this the abundant life, the salt of the earth and light of the world?

Here is a trustworthy saying: If anyone sets his heart on being an overseer, he desires a noble task. [168]

---

[167] Mark 14:6.   [168] 1 Tim. 3:1.

Some people have said that a *desire* for the ministry of tending the flock of God is a *qualification* for that work. This may be going too far; there may be things a person *should* desire but *doesn't* desire, and that is another problem. But Paul seems to assume that a qualified man will indeed desire the noble ministry of overseeing the relationships, responsibilities, and needs existing among the members of the Christian community. Like any other idol, personal fulfillment is a bad thing when it becomes the ultimate goal of life's pursuit; but it is a good thing when God grants personal fulfillment as the "natural by-product" of faithful discipleship:

> *"For whoever wants to save his life will lose it, but whoever loses his life for me and for the gospel will save it."* [169]

Every genuine disciple of Christ has removed "self" from the throne of his or her life. The motivating principle is no longer egocentricity; it is the love of God, revealed in Christ and communicated by the Holy Spirit. In the setting of this unselfish love for God and man, one's first concern is the kingdom of God, the doing of God's will. When God and His will are our primary concern, God Himself will see to all of our needs—including personal fulfillment. *It is safe to enjoy oneself in Christ,* because our priorities are right when Christ is ruling our hearts.

A ministry should "fit" correctly; it should be comfortable, not cramping. Body members should function in the place for which God has designed and equipped them— and not feel guilty about being who they are in Christ. A

---

[169]Mark 8:35.

foot should be a foot, and should not be intimidated into trying to function as a hand. What you *desire* to do, *like* to do, and are *willing* to do will ultimately be the ministry you will *enjoy.*

It is my hope that each member of the body of Christ will come to appreciate his or her own unique personality, ministry, talents, and gifts. It is my prayer that each local expression of the body of Christ will provide an environment of appreciation for each member, and for each member's ministry. God, in His wisdom, has called many different members together in one body.

In the midst of a world that desperately needs to see the beauty of a life of love, acceptance, and belonging, the church must live as the body of Christ.

APPENDIX:

MUTUAL MINISTRIES OF LOVE

I have here catalogued the New Testament references which explicitly call for "one another" ministries and relationships in the body of Christ. These references describe a life-style, not a mere set of functions. They presuppose a close-knit community of believers in which covenant relationship and responsibilities toward God and man are understood and honored by every member on a local level. The Greek word commonly translated "one another" is *allelon*, usually meaning "one of another," "one from another," or "one toward another." There are about six passages where the "one another" idea is translated from the plural of the personal pronoun *heautou*, meaning "to yourselves" or "among yourselves." These will be designated by an asterisk (*).

1. *Serve* one another (John 13:14; Gal. 5:13; contrast Gal. 5:15, 17).

2. *Love* one another (John 13:34-45; 15:12, 17; Rom. 13:8; 1 Thess. 3:12; 4:9; 2 Thess. 1:3; 1 Peter 1:22; 1 John 3:11, 23; 4:7, 11-12; also, 2 John 5).

3. *Encourage* one another (Rom. 1:12; Heb. 10:25).

4. *Have brotherly affection* toward one another (Rom. 12:10).

5. *Be impartial* toward one another (Rom. 12:16; compare James 2:1-13).

6. *Do not judge* one another (Rom. 14:13; compare Matt. 7:1-5; James 4:11-12).

7. *Edify* one another (Rom. 14:19; Eph. 4:29).

8. *Be like-minded* towards one another (Rom. 15:5; compare Phil. 2:1-5).

9. *Receive* one another (Rom. 15:7; compare Rom. 14:1).

10. *Admonish* one another (Rom. 15:14).

11. *Greet* one another (Rom. 16:16; compare 1 Peter 5:14; 1 Cor. 16:20; 2 Cor. 13:12).

12. *Do not defraud* one another (1 Cor. 7:5; compare 1 Thess. 4:3-6; Heb. 13:4).

13. *Wait* for one another (1 Cor. 11:33).

14. *Care* for one another (1 Cor. 12:25).

15. *Bear burdens* for one another (Gal. 6:2).

16. *Bear with* one another (Eph. 4:2; compare Col. 3:13).

17. *Be kind and tenderhearted* toward one another (Eph. 4:32; 1 Thess. 5:15).

18. *Submit* to one another (Eph. 5:21; 1 Peter 5:5).

19. *Esteem* one another (Phil. 2:3).

20. *Do not lie* to one another (Col. 3:9; compare Eph. 4:25).

21. *Comfort* one another (1 Thess. 4:18; 5:11; compare 2 Cor. 1:3-7).

22. *Motivate* one another (Heb. 10:24).

23. *Do not slander* one another (James 4:11; compare Eph. 4:29).

24. *Do not grumble against* one another (James 5:9).

25. *Confess to* and *pray for* one another (James 5:16).

26. *Be hospitable* to one another (1 Peter 4:9).

27. *Have fellowship* with one another (1 John 1:7; compare Acts 2:42).

*28. *Do not go to law* with one another (1 Cor. 6:7).

*29. *Forgive* one another (Eph. 4:32; Col 3:13).

*30. *Teach and admonish* one another with songs (Col. 3:16).

*31. *Exhort* one another (Heb. 3:13).

*32. *Minister to* one another (1 Peter 4:10).

*33. *Speak to* one another with songs (Eph. 5:19).

SCRIPTURE INDEX
(Bold type shows direct quotations.)

303

306

ONE BODY

You and I are different
But we love the same Lord
We express ourselves in very different ways
Baptized by One Spirit
Through the gospel, born again
If you'll open up your heart
You'll hear Him say:

We are One Body
One Body
We're the Body of the Lord
And it's such a shame
When we tear that Body down
One Body!
One Body!
Can't you see that's what we are
And what God has joined
Let no man tear apart.

I need you, and you need me
That's the way it's meant to be
When one man cries another man sheds a tear
A common joy, a common love
And a common cup to drink
Let's remember, we're communing
With the Lord.

Now, you are the Body of Christ
And each of you a part
And the gifts you have are for the common good
So don't forget to use them
To serve your fellow man
To build him up in the atmosphere of love.

©1988 Keith Luker